Elegant Meals
with Inexpensive Meats

Created and designed
by the editorial staff
of ORTHO Books

Written by
Cynthia Scheer

Art direction by
Linda Hinrichs

Designed by
Jennie Chien

Photography by
Fred Lyon

Photographic styling by
Sara Slavin

Illustrations by
Ellen Blonder

Elegant Meals
with Inexpensive Meats

See the inside back cover for a metric conversion chart.

Introducing Inexpensive Meats

Economy cuts are more plentiful and varied than you might suppose. And you can find them wherever you shop for meat and poultry. This books shows you how to transform them into elegant meals.

It has been said there are enough cuts and kinds of meat to serve a different meat dish every single day of the year. Better yet, the greater proportion of them are the less expensive ones.

An economist might explain this fortunate phenomenon in terms of the law of supply and demand. A *home* economist gets more specific: the loin and rib sections of beef, pork and lamb account for but a small part of the available meat from those animals; they are also in the greatest demand, and hence command the highest prices, because of their familiarity and dependable tenderness.

Doesn't that bring out the possibly latent but much-praised native American thrift-conscious streak in us all! Knowing that an amazing variety of less costly meat can be found in any supermarket meat counter—a source of good flavor and most welcome dinnertime variety to boot—is a challenge too inviting to decline.

The recipes in this book will lead you to discover there's more to thrifty meat buying than hamburger and hot dogs. Of course, you'll find recipes for these standbys, too. They wouldn't be favorites unless they tasted good.

Getting the Most From Your Meat Dollar

The best buys in the meat counter usually require some know-how from you, the customer. To get the most from the meat you purchase, it's fundamental that it be cooked using a method that makes it pleasingly tender, juicy and flavorful.

This book is divided into chapters based on different methods of cooking: dry-heat cooking, such as roasting, broiling, pan-broiling and grilling or barbecuing; and moist-heat techniques such as stewing, braising and soup making. Within each style, appropriate cuts of meat have been

You can learn some of the knacks of a traditional meat dealer like Anthony Iacopi of San Francisco.

selected. Some of the choices may surprise you because they depart from tradition and reveal more versatility than you might suspect. For example, there's a tender steak you can broil—two of them, in fact—hidden in the mundane blade-cut chuck roast usually cooked as a pot roast. (See page 7.)

Learning to identify cuts of meat and their potential as main dishes your family and guests will enjoy will be easier if you familiarize yourself with the basic retail cuts, which can be seen in the chart, page 6. There are just seven important areas to learn.

The *loin* (short loin and sirloin) and *rib* cuts are usually the most costly, whether beef, pork, veal or lamb. This is the area from which come the expensive steaks, beef fillet and pork tenderloin, standing rib roast, rack of lamb and center-cut pork chops.

Most of the recipes in this cookbook are for the cuts of meat from before, behind and below the rib and loin, where the bargains are. Starting at the front end, some of the consistently lowest cost meats are from the *blade* cuts—shoulder and chuck from beef and Boston butt from pork.

Three of the consistently best meat values are blade-cut chuck roast, whole chicken and full-cut round steak.

Below this area are the *arm* cuts, which include beef shanks and short ribs and the picnic shoulder roast of pork. Just behind the arm is the *brisket* and *breast* area, notable for the corned beef it produces, pork spareribs and veal and lamb breast. In pork, the boneless meat from this section is cured and smoked to become bacon.

Behind the loin is the *leg* or *round*. In beef it contains the familiar round steak, which is comprised of three quite different portions (each with its own fascinating potential) as well as rump roasts, the sirloin tip and, of course, oxtails. In pork the leg is smoked for ham, in lamb the entire leg may be sold as leg of lamb.

It should be pointed out that a low price-per-pound on meat doesn't necessarily guarantee economy. Keep in mind the amount of *cooked lean* meat it provides, as well. From cuts with little or no fat or bone you can expect three to four servings per pound. Cuts with a medium amount of bone (poultry falls into this category, as do many chops and steaks) provide two to three servings per pound. From cuts with a high proportion of fat and bone—such as spareribs, beef and lamb shanks, short ribs and premium steaks such as porterhouse and T-bone—you will get just one to two servings per pound.

What about quality?.All meat processed in plants which sell their products across state lines in the United States is inspected for wholesomeness. Most of it is also graded for quality. The top grades in beef are USDA Prime, USDA Choice and USDA Good.

Most of the beef graded "prime" is found in restaurants and specialty meat markets. The grade most widely sold at retail is "choice." Below it on this quality scale is "good" grade beef. Relatively tender, somewhat leaner than the higher grades, but lacking some of their juiciness and flavor, this quality beef is sold by many supermarket chains under their own quality designation rather than a USDA grade name.

Beef Chart

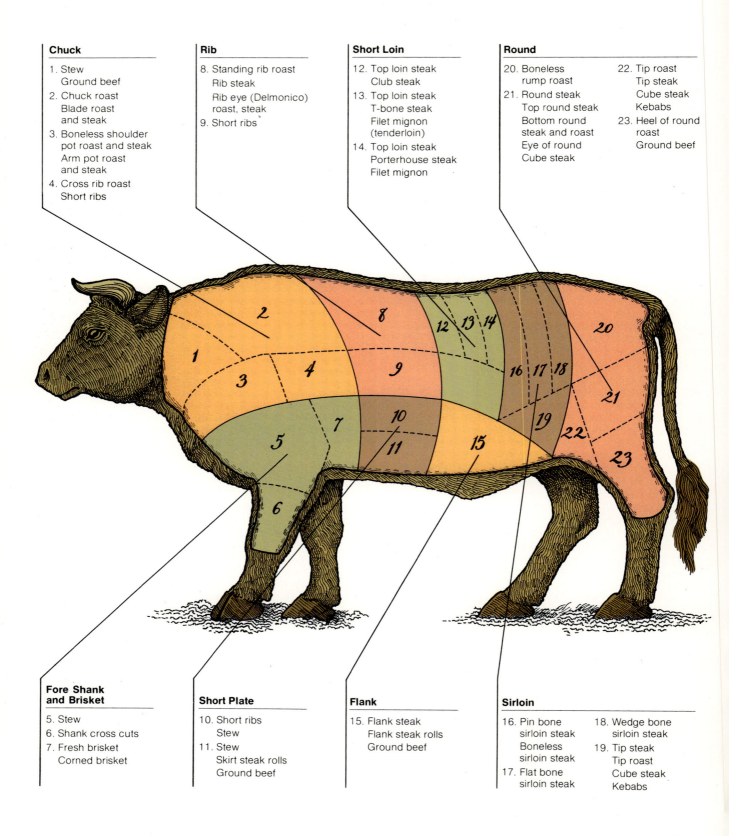

Chuck

1. Stew
   Ground beef
2. Chuck roast
   Blade roast
   and steak
3. Boneless shoulder
   pot roast and steak
   Arm pot roast
   and steak
4. Cross rib roast
   Short ribs

Rib

8. Standing rib roast
   Rib steak
   Rib eye (Delmonico)
   roast, steak
9. Short ribs

Short Loin

12. Top loin steak
    Club steak
13. Top loin steak
    T-bone steak
    Filet mignon
    (tenderloin)
14. Top loin steak
    Porterhouse steak
    Filet mignon

Round

20. Boneless
    rump roast
21. Round steak
    Top round steak
    Bottom round
    steak and roast
    Eye of round
    Cube steak
22. Tip roast
    Tip steak
    Cube steak
    Kebabs
23. Heel of round
    roast
    Ground beef

**Fore Shank
and Brisket**

5. Stew
6. Shank cross cuts
7. Fresh brisket
   Corned brisket

Short Plate

10. Short ribs
    Stew
11. Stew
    Skirt steak rolls
    Ground beef

Flank

15. Flank steak
    Flank steak rolls
    Ground beef

Sirloin

16. Pin bone
    sirloin steak
    Boneless
    sirloin steak
17. Flat bone
    sirloin steak
18. Wedge bone
    sirloin steak
19. Tip steak
    Tip roast
    Cube steak
    Kebabs

All meat animals can be broken down into seven basic sections. The sections indicated on the beef chart above are typical. Blade cuts, such as chuck roasts, are found in the sections numbered 1 through 4; arm cuts, 5 and 6; brisket and breast, 7, 10 and 11. The most expensive parts of the animal are in the rib (8 and 9), short loin (12 through 14) and sirloin (16 through 19) areas. Good values can also be found in the leg or round (20 through 23).

Exploring Some Standard Meat Counter Specials

One way to get excited about hidden meat values is to discover them yourself. Here are a few tricks you can learn to perform with some of the meats your supermarket features as low-priced specials almost any week of the year—chuck roast, round steak and whole body frying chicken.

Chuck Roast

A blade-cut chuck roast takes its name from the knife-shaped blade bone that bisects the top third from left to right.

There are really three distinct meaty parts. The flatiron muscle, the portion at the left in the illustration below, is tender enough to stir-fry quickly or for a speedy sauté such as *Beef Stroganoff* on page 34. The center part is the least tender, the section that dictates long slow cooking in liquid; a good use of it is the *Burgundy Beef Stew* on page 63.

In the remaining third of this roast is that hidden but very tender steak, actually an extension of the rib eye. From a 5-pound blade-cut chuck roast you can make two steaks, cutting the meat horizontally. You can cook the steaks in many elegant ways, all of them as quick as they are delicious (see chapter 3 for *Steak with Tangy Herb Butter,* as well as *Mustard and Pepper Steak, Steak and Onions for Two* and *Gypsy-Style Steak*).

When you see this chuck roast at a special price, buy two, bring them home and divide them along the natu-

Less costly beef offers infinite possibilities for elegant meals.

ral boundaries shown below.

Separate the meat from the bones—and be sure to save the bones. There is a recipe for a meaty soup stock that can also be reduced to a richly flavored meat gelatin to use for flavoring gravies and sauces on page 10. Freeze the bones until you have enough to make broth.

Package and label the different sections from the roast, and freeze any meat you can't use within three or four days.

Round Steak

Boneless or bone-in, full-cut round steak is another beef cut frequently featured at a price that makes it a very good buy. This cut has three quite obvious divisions. When you consider that each is usually sold at a much higher price per pound, it is apparent that it is well worth the slight effort of separating them yourself.

Two of the three muscles in the round, the eye and the bottom round, are fairly compact. Although the eye of round is a handsome-looking cut of meat, it is the least tender part of the round. Handled cleverly it makes a steak to cook quickly (as in the *Elegant Eye of Round Steaks,* page 33) or braise in a savory liquid (*Braised Eye of Round Steaks,* page 66).

The bottom round, especially, is coarse and requires long slow cooking in liquid to become tender. It is the portion of the round that gives this cut its Swiss steak associations. But for two less familiar treatments, try *Round Steak and Kidney Beans* or *Sauerbraten-Style Steak Strips* (pages 71 and 64).

The top round is the most tender and also the largest portion. Thick cuts, particularly if graded "choice," can be broiled to the rare or medium-rare stage very satisfactorily. If you find that top round usually isn't tender enough when broiled or cooked by other dry-heat methods (grilling, pan-frying, barbecuing), use a marinade or an unseasoned meat tenderizer. Some specific suggestions for lean, reasonably priced and versatile top round include *Shish Kebab Sauté* and *Beef Fondue* (pages 34 and 35).

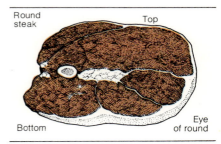
With or without round bone, full-cut round steak is usually a good buy.

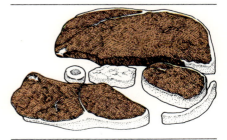
Separated into its three muscles: top round, the most tender portion; bottom round, to cook slowly in liquid; and eye of round, which needs careful attention to be tender.

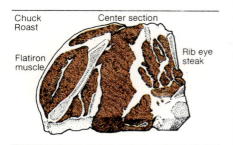
Thrifty blade-cut chuck roast.

Stir-fry or sauté tender meat at left, stew center section, cut rib eye into two steaks; save bones for soup.

Whole Chicken

Even when chicken doesn't have a special price tag, whole birds are less expensive than those that have been cut up. Buy chicken in this form and you'll also have a choice of ways to use it. Depending on the size, you can roast it whole, with or without stuffing; cut it in halves to bake, broil or cook on the barbecue; quarter it for neat, meaty one-serving portions, or cut it into conventional pieces.

What's more, you'll get giblets and some bones such as the neck and backbone to save in the freezer to make broth later. Freeze the livers until you have enough to make the luscious hors d'oeuvre spread on page 11.

Boneless chicken breasts are another choice cut that always commands a premium price when you buy them separately. With very little practice, you can learn to bone them yourself for some very impressive dishes.

You can cut up the versatile and economical whole frying chicken so many ways—halves, quarters, pieces or elegant boneless breasts. It's easy when you follow the step-by-step instructions.

How to Cut Up a Chicken

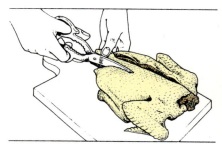

Cutting out back bone

Place chicken breast down on board. Use knife or kitchen scissors to remove back bone by cutting along both sides.

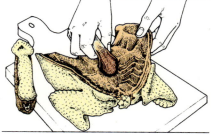

Removing keel bone from breast

Reach inside to remove the keel bone that separates the two sides of the breast. Loosen dark hard part and flexible white portion with your fingers or a small knife; pull out in one or two pieces. Save bones for broth (page 11).

Can there be a more versatile or popular food than chicken? Roast it, simmer it, use it in casseroles or soup.

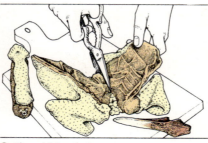

Cutting chicken halves

For chicken halves, cut between breasts where the keel bone was removed. From small birds (2½ pounds or less), each half makes a generous single serving to bake, broil or barbecue (see Piquant Roast Chicken Halves, page 23).

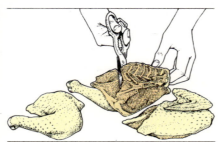

Separating halves into quarters

To cut chicken quarters, lift up on rib bones of breast section to see where it divides from leg-thigh part (meat is a little darker). Cut from side to side below bottom rib bones. Quarters from 3-pound (and larger) chickens can be baked, broiled, barbecued or cooked in delicious sauces.

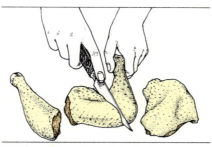

Chicken pieces: drumsticks first

Cutting a whole chicken into familiar pieces is easy once you've gone this far, and learning to do it yourself is well worth the trouble. You now have two leg-thigh quarters and two breast-wing quarters. Wiggle the drumstick to find the joint, then cut through it (between the bones, if you can find the right spot) to separate the legs from the thighs.

Finally you will be left with chicken breasts with wings attached. Often, in preparing elegant Continental entrées, the two smaller wing joints can be removed and the breast boned, leaving just the large wing joint with the bone in. But for day-to-day family dishes,

you will probably proceed from here by simply cutting off the entire wing at the joint where it is attached to the breast. Save the wings for soup, or try Sweet-and-Sour Chicken Wings (page 41) for a colorful supper dish.

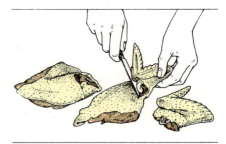

To cut wings away from breasts

How to Bone a Chicken Breast
Everytime you cut up a thrifty whole chicken, you get two plump breast pieces to use in some of the most elegant dishes of all. This is the way to bone them.

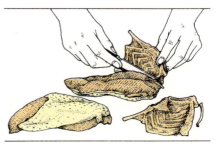

Cut out rib cage

First remove rib bones from each breast half. Insert tip of a small sharp knife under the long, bottom rib bone. Work it under the bone and cut it away from the meat (pull up on the bones; push and scrape the meat downward and free.) Keep cutting around the outer edge of the breast to and then through the shoulder joint to remove the entire rib cage.

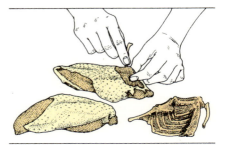

Strip meat from wishbone

Working from the ends, scrape meat away from each side of the wishbone; cut and lift it out. Turn meat over and pull away the skin with your fingers. Reserve the bones and skin for broth.

Cut-up chickens, packed and frozen in halves, quarters or pieces, are a boon to the busy cook. Poultry should only be kept frozen 6 to 8 months.

Even inexpensive meats make up a big part of your food budget. So after you buy meat, be sure to store it properly until you are ready to cook it.

Storing the Meat You Buy

Meat and poultry are perishable foods, so be sure to buy no more than you can store and use efficiently during the time they will keep in the refrigerator or freezer.

Fresh beef, veal, pork and lamb can be kept in a 38° to 48°F refrigerator for two to four days; chicken and ground meats should be used sooner, within one to two days.

Meats keep better if they are allowed to dry out a little on the surface. So keep refrigerator wrappings loose. You can use foil, waxed paper or the original supermarket prepackaging.

More care is needed for freezing meat and poultry. The chart in the back section of this cookbook gives you guidelines for how long they can be kept in the freezer. For best quality, your freezer should freeze meat fast and then hold it with a minimum of temperature fluctuation at 0°F or colder. Otherwise, large ice crystals form, rupturing the meat fibers and allowing juices to escape when the meat is thawed.

To prevent drying and those tough patches called "freezer burn," meat and poultry should be securely packaged in a moisture-vaporproof material such as coated freezer paper or heavy foil. Keep some small press-on labels in the kitchen so you can identify and date the meat as it is frozen.

Defrost frozen meat and poultry in their original freezer wrappings, larger cuts preferably in the refrigerator, allowing about 5 hours per pound. Defrosting at room temperature, which is only recommended for smaller cuts, will take about 2 to 3 hours per pound.

Stocking Your Freezer With a Side of Beef

One economical way to buy beef is to purchase it a side (a half) or quarter at a time, packaged, labeled and frozen. If you have a capacious freezer, you will have a ready supply. And also, you can work with the meat dealer to get just the cuts you want—steaks if you're usually in a hurry or cooking for one or two, roasts if you have a big family or entertain frequently. A cooperative butcher will divide the chuck or round into the various muscles according to their tenderness (the sort of thing shown on a smaller scale on page 7.)

The price per pound you pay is based on the hanging weight of the entire side or quarter. There is about a 27 to 28 percent weight loss by the time that it is broken down into retail cuts you specify, due to loss of moisture, bone and trimmed fat.

The hindquarter, which includes the loin section, is usually more costly than a forequarter (mostly rib and chuck). From a 300 to 320-pound side of beef, figure on about 17 percent loin cuts, 9 percent rib cuts, 22 percent round, 26 percent chuck, and the remaining 26 percent flank, plate, shanks and suet.

Save the Bones— and the Chicken Livers

When you bring home meat or poultry containing bones, you might as well make the most of them. After all, you've paid for them. Save them in a sturdy plastic bag in the freezer until enough have accumulated to make a rich full-flavored broth. It will have so many uses: liquid for stews, spaghetti sauce and gravy; for cooking rice when you make a pilaf; the beginning of a sturdy full-meal soup.

Notice how many of your favorite recipes include a can of beef or chicken broth and you'll quickly realize how worthwhile it is to make your own. Although a good rich broth needs to cook for a long time, it does so unattended while you spend the hours on something else.

Rich Beef Broth or Beef Concentrate

Bones from several chuck roasts are especially fine for making this flavorful beef broth. If you wish, you can cook it further to make a concentrated meat jelly; French chefs call it *glace de viande* and wouldn't be without it to enrich sauces for meat.

The meat concentrate is reduced until it becomes a rubbery gelatin when cooled. Divide it among small jars; freeze all but the one you keep in the refrigerator for day-to-day use. About 2 teaspoons dissolved in a cup of hot water is the equivalent of a beef bouillon cube or 1 teaspoon of powdered beef stock base.

10 pounds (approximately) meaty beef bones
3 medium carrots
3 large onions
2 stalks celery, with leaves, chopped
1 can (1 lb.) tomatoes
Water

1. Place bones in a large open roasting pan in a single layer. Sprinkle with one of the carrots, sliced, and one of the onions, thickly sliced. Bake in a 450° oven, uncovered, for about 30 minutes until meat and bones are well browned.

2. Transfer the mixture to a large deep kettle (at least 12-quart size). Add remaining carrots and onions, chopped, celery and tomatoes, coarsely chopped, and their liquid. Add water to cover bones. Bring to boiling, cover, reduce heat and simmer between 18 to 24 hours.

3. Strain the soup to remove bones and vegetables. Return the broth to cooking pot. Simmer, uncovered, until it is reduced by about half. Pour the broth through several thicknesses of dampened cheesecloth or a clean muslin or linen kitchen towel into a large bowl. Cover and chill.

4. Remove and discard fat. To use as beef broth, reheat and season lightly with salt. Freeze for long-term storage.

Makes 2½ to 3 quarts rich broth.

5. For beef concentrate, place the broth in a 3 to 4-quart saucepan after it has been chilled and the fat removed (broth will be firm and gelatinous at this stage). Bring to a gentle boil and cook, uncovered, stirring occasionally until it is thick enough to make a syrupy-looking coating on the spoon and boils all over in large shiny bubbles. You should have about 2 cups. Cool, then pour into several small jars and refrigerate (for up to 2 or 3 weeks) or freeze. Use about 2 teaspoons per cup of water to make regular-strength beef broth.

Golden Chicken Broth

For all the jokes about chicken soup, it *is* a useful ingredient to have stored in your freezer.

5 pounds bony chicken pieces (backs, necks and/or wings)
1 medium onion, chopped
1 carrot, sliced
1 stalk celery, with leaves, chopped
3 sprigs parsley
¼ teaspoon crumbled thyme
½ bay leaf
Dash marjoram
3 quarts cold water
Salt

1. In a large deep kettle (8 to 10-quart size) place chicken pieces, vegetables, parsley, thyme, bay leaf, marjoram and cold water. Bring the liquid to boiling, then reduce heat and simmer, covered, for 3½ to 4 hours, until the broth has a rich chicken flavor.

2. Strain the broth, discarding bones and vegetables. Return the broth to

Simmer beef bones in a big pot to make a savory broth. For flavoring sauces and gravies, you can cook it until it is reduced to a rich brown meat jelly.

the kettle and simmer it, uncovered, until it is reduced to about 2 quarts, about 1 hour. Salt to taste.

3. If possible, chill the broth overnight, then skim off and discard fat. Freeze, or chill and use within 3 to 4 days.

Makes about 2 quarts.

Save-the-Chicken-Livers Spread

Every time you cook chicken, put the liver into a small container for freezing. It doesn't take long to save enough livers for this excellent paté to serve with crisp rye crackers or melba toast.

½ pound (about ¾ cup) chicken livers, thawed if frozen
Water
3 tablespoons dry sherry
¼ cup *each* butter and margarine, softened
1 shallot, finely chopped, *or* 1 tablespoon finely chopped onion
1 teaspoon Dijon-style mustard
½ teaspoon salt
¼ teaspoon nutmeg
Dash cayenne

1. Place chicken livers in a saucepan and cover with water. Bring to a gentle boil, cover, reduce heat and simmer until tender, 10 to 12 minutes; drain. Place in blender with sherry; whirl until smooth. Cool slightly.

2. Transfer to a bowl and mix in remaining ingredients. Beat until fluffy and well combined. Cover and chill several hours to blend flavors. Soften at room temperature for 1 hour.

Makes about 1 cup.

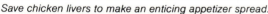

Save chicken livers to make an enticing appetizer spread.

Affordable Roasts

For inexpensive elegance from the oven, discover the less costly cuts of beef, pork, lamb, veal and poultry that make impressive guest dinners and family feasts.

Often the traditional meal for company or a large family gathering features a roast. Some of the most popular ones are a ham, a leg of lamb, a standing rib roast of beef, a pork loin roast or a plump turkey. However, if you are watching your food budget, all but the last are usually quite costly.

Take heart: there are plenty of other affordable roasts of meat and poultry that can be just as festive and satisfying as conventional favorites.

First of all, what is a roast? It is a cut of meat or poultry cooked in the oven by dry heat (that is, without the addition of moisture), uncovered. Most roasts are cooked in a shallow pan to permit good air circulation for even heat penetration.

A roast is usually placed fat side up so that the fat that melts during cooking will baste the meat as it drains. A rack or trivet in the bottom of the pan holds the meat out of its drippings.

For most roasts, a constant moderate oven temperature—usually 325°—produces the juiciest meat with the least shrinkage. At this setting, heat penetrates all the way to the center of even a large roast before the outside becomes dry or burned. You may have heard about searing meat at a high temperature "to seal in the juices." Actually, repeated tests have shown that, on the contrary, meat cooked this way is *less* juicy. The drippings may produce a browner gravy, but there is also drier meat and a spattered oven.

An absolutely basic piece of equipment for roasting is a meat thermometer, preferably a mercury one. Inserted so that the bulb is in the center of the largest muscle without touching fat or bone, it shows the temperature of the thickest part of the roast—the only reliable indicator that the meat has cooked to your preference.

Roasting timetables like the one on page 15 can help you estimate the time a roast must be put in the oven. But if you've ever agonized over a gray beef roast that should have been pink, or an outwardly glorious holiday turkey that resisted the carver's best efforts, you will appreciate an accurate meat thermometer.

Beef

Italian-Style Roast Beef with Baked Vegetables

A fairly lean yet juicy boneless rolled roast from the shoulder or chuck, known as a cross rib roast or a shoulder clod roast, often carries a moderate price tag. It will be most tender if cooked to a rare 135° to 145°. Baked with onions, carrots and new potatoes and accompanied by a salad and dessert, it provides a satisfying meal for family or guests.

  ⅓ cup olive oil or salad oil
  ¼ teaspoon crumbled oregano
  2 cloves garlic, slivered
  2 pounds small new potatoes
  3 medium onions, cut in eighths
  6 large carrots, cut lengthwise in quarters
4½ to 5-pound boneless rolled cross rib roast
  Coarsely ground pepper
  Chopped parsley and lemon wedges

1. In a shallow roasting pan about 10 by 15 inches, mix oil, oregano and garlic. Peel potatoes completely, if you wish, or peel a 1-inch-wide strip around center of each. Add potatoes, onions and carrots to oil mixture, stirring to coat well. Move vegetables to ends of pan.

2. Place roast, fat side up, in center of pan. Sprinkle with pepper. Roast, uncovered, in a 325° oven, for about 1½ to 2 hours, turning potatoes once, until vegetables are tender and meat thermometer inserted in center of thickest part of roast registers 135° (rare) to 145° (medium-rare to medium).

3. Slice meat and serve with parsley-sprinkled vegetables, with pan juices spooned over and lemon wedges to squeeze over each serving.

Makes 8 to 10 servings.

Italian-style cross rib roast bakes with vegetables.
Far left: Affordable roasts of meat and poultry can be festive for parties.

Soy and Sesame Roast

A boneless rump roast is both lean and compact. That means it can be roasted to tender juiciness with standard dry heat methods, but for extra tenderness, marinate it first and then cook it to a rare 130° to 135°. Accompany this one with rice sprinkled with sliced green onions and any extra toasted sesame seeds.

⅔ cup soy sauce
2 tablespoons honey
½ teaspoon ground ginger
2 cloves garlic, minced or pressed
⅓ cup dry sherry
4 to 4½-pound boneless rolled
**   rump roast**
2 tablespoons toasted
**   sesame seeds**
**   (directions follow)**

1. Gradually stir soy sauce into honey in a small bowl. Blend in ginger, garlic and sherry. Place roast in a bowl or deep casserole just large enough to hold it comfortably. Pour on marinade. Cover and refrigerate for 8 hours or overnight, turning meat occasionally.

2. Remove meat, reserving marinade. Place roast on a rack, fat side up, in a shallow roasting pan. Sprinkle with toasted sesame seeds. Roast in a 325° oven, drizzling occasionally with marinade, for 1½ to 2 hours, until meat thermometer registers 130° to 135° (rare).

3. Slice thinly and serve.

Makes 8 to 10 servings.

Toasted Sesame Seeds: Spread in a shallow pan; bake in a 350° oven, stirring occasionally, until lightly browned, 8 to 10 minutes.

Chuck Roast Marinated in Beer

A marinade containing acid in some form—lemon juice, vinegar or wine—can tenderize as well as flavor some of the less tender cuts of meat. If you doubt that, give this lemon-beer marinated chuck roast a try—but *only* if you like rare meat; cooked beyond the rare stage this roast won't be tender.

This dish is an exception to the rule of roasting in a 325° oven: because this type of chuck roast is much broader than it is thick, a hotter oven does a better job of browning the outside of the meat while the inside stays rare and juicy.

4½ to 5-pound blade-cut or
**   seven-bone chuck roast, fat**
**   trimmed**
1 cup beer
½ cup salad oil
2 tablespoons lemon juice
1 clove garlic, minced or pressed
1 bay leaf
¾ teaspoon salt
½ teaspoon *each* pepper, dry
**   mustard, rosemary, oregano and**
**   thyme**

1. Place roast in a shallow baking dish. Thoroughly combine remaining ingredients; pour over roast. Cover and refrigerate for 4 to 6 hours or overnight, turning meat occasionally.

2. Place roast on rack in an uncovered roasting pan; brush with marinade. Roast in a 450° oven for 35 to 55 minutes, until meat thermometer registers 135° (rare) to 145° (medium-rare to medium). Carve as shown below.

Makes 6 to 8 servings.

Beer makes a lively marinade for an economical blade-cut chuck roast, also seasoned with lemon juice, garlic and herbs. Roast the meat in a hot oven, then carve it as you would a big tender, rare steak.

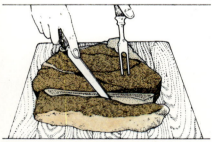

To carve, cut close to bones to divide chuck roast into several large pieces.

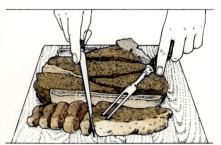

Then slice each section across the grain and serve, discarding bones.

Sirloin Tip Roast with Oven-Browned Potatoes and Stuffed Mushroom Caps

One of the most elegant of the less expensive beef oven roasts is the sirloin tip. Lean and tender, it comes from the portion of the round that lies next to the sirloin. For a really special dinner, serve this handsome roast with crusty potatoes baked in the meat drippings, accompanied by savory stuffed mushrooms.

Accompany the roast with asparagus spears and dinner rolls. For the salad course, toss mixed greens with blue cheese dressing and sprinkle with crisp bacon crumbles.

1 clove garlic, thinly slivered
4½ to 5-pound boneless rolled sirloin tip roast
½ teaspoon crumbled tarragon
Seasoned pepper
6 medium baking potatoes (about 2¼ lbs.)
3 tablespoons salad oil
1 teaspoon seasoned salt
Stuffed Mushroom Caps (recipe follows)

1. Insert garlic slivers in thin slashes cut in fat covering roast. Place roast, fat side up, in center of a shallow roasting pan, about 10 by 15 inches. Sprinkle evenly with tarragon and seasoned pepper. Place in a 325° oven.

2. Meanwhile, peel and quarter potatoes. Mix with oil and seasoned salt. Arrange around roast in a single layer; drizzle with any remaining oil mixture. Replace in oven. Turn potatoes after 45 minutes.

3. Continue roasting until meat thermometer registers 135° (rare) to 145° (medium-rare to medium) and potatoes are tender, crusty and golden— 1½ to 2 hours. Slice meat thinly and serve with potatoes and mushrooms.

Makes 8 to 10 servings.

Stuffed Mushroom Caps: Remove stems from 12 medium mushrooms; chop stems finely. Sauté caps briefly in 2 tablespoons butter or margarine; remove from pan. Add 1 tablespoon more butter, and in it cook chopped mushroom stems, ¼ cup finely chopped smoked pork shoulder picnic or ham and 2 tablespoons finely chopped onion. Remove from heat and mix in 2 tablespoons chopped parsley, ⅛ teaspoon crumbled tarragon and ¼ cup *each* soft bread crumbs and shredded Monterey jack cheese. Mound stuffing mixture into mushroom caps. Arrange in a single layer in a buttered baking dish. Place in oven with roast during the last 15 minutes, until heated through and lightly browned.

Roasting Timetable

	Weight (Pounds)	Oven Temperature	Internal Meat Temperature	Cooking Time (Minutes per lb)
Beef				
Rib	6 to 8	300°–325°F	140°F (rare)	23 to 25
(Ribs which measure			160°F (medium)	27 to 30
6 to 7 inches from			170°F (well)	32 to 35
chine bone to tip	4 to 6	300°–325°F	140°F (rare)	26 to 32
of rib.)			160°F (medium)	34 to 38
			170°F (well)	40 to 42
Rolled rib	5 to 7	300°–325°F	140°F (rare)	32
			160°F (medium)	38
			170°F (well)	48
Rib eye (Delmonico)	4 to 6	350°F	140°F (rare)	18 to 20
			160°F (medium)	20 to 22
			170°F (well)	22 to 24
Tenderloin, whole	4 to 6	425°F	140°F (rare)	45 to 60 (total)
Tenderloin, half	2 to 3	425°F	140°F (rare)	45 to 60 (total)
Boneless rolled rump	4 to 6	300°–325°F	150°F–170°F	25 to 30
Tip	3½ to 4	300°–325°F	140°F–170°F	35 to 40
	4 to 6	300°–325°F	140°F–170°F	30 to 35
Veal				
Leg	5 to 8	300°–325°F	170°F	25 to 35
Loin	4 to 6	300°–325°F	170°F	30 to 35
Rib (rack)	3 to 5	300°–325°F	170°F	35 to 40
Boneless shoulder	4 to 6	300°–325°F	170°F	40 to 45
Pork, Fresh				
Loin				
Center	3 to 5	325°–350°F	170°F	30 to 35
Half	5 to 7	325°–350°F	170°F	35 to 40
Blade loin or sirloin	3 to 4	325°–350°F	170°F	40 to 45
Boneless double	3 to 5	325°–350°F	170°F	35 to 40
Arm picnic shoulder	5 to 8	325°–350°F	170°F	30 to 35
Boneless	3 to 5	325°–350°F	170°F	35 to 40
Cushion	3 to 5	325°–350°F	170°F	30 to 35
Blade Boston shoulder	4 to 6	325°–350°F	170°F	40 to 45
Leg (fresh ham)				
Whole (bone in)	12 to 16	325°–350°F	170°F	22 to 26
Whole (boneless)	10 to 14	325°–350°F	170°F	24 to 28
Half (bone in)	5 to 8	325°–350°F	170°F	35 to 40
Spareribs		325°–350°F	Well done	1½ to 2½ hrs (total)
Pork, Smoked				
Ham (cook-before-eating)				
Whole	10 to 14	300°–325°F	160°F	18 to 20
Half	5 to 7	300°–325°F	160°F	22 to 25
Shank or rump portion	3 to 4	300°–325°F	160°F	35 to 40
Ham (fully cooked)	10 to 14	325°F	140°F	15
Half	5 to 7	325°F	140°F	18 to 24
Arm picnic shoulder	5 to 8	300°–325°F	170°F	35
Shoulder roll	2 to 3	300°–325°F	170°F	35 to 40
Canadian-style bacon	2 to 4	325°F	160°F	35 to 40
Lamb				
Leg	5 to 8	300°–325°F	175°F–180°F	30 to 35
Shoulder	4 to 6	300°–325°F	175°F–180°F	30 to 35
Boneless	3 to 5	300°–325°F	175°F–180°F	40 to 45
Cushion	3 to 5	300°–325°F	175°F–180°F	30 to 35
Rib	1½ to 3	375°F	170°F–180°F	35 to 45

	Weight	Oven Temperature	Time per lb. (Without Stuffing)	Cooking Time*
Chicken	1½ lbs	400°F	40 min	1 hour
	2 lbs	400°F	35 min	1 hr 10 min
	2½ lbs	375°F	30 min	1 hr 15 min
	3 lbs	375°F	30 min	1 hr 30 min
	3½ lbs	375°F	30 min	1 hr 45 min
	4 lbs	375°F	30 min	2 hours
	4½ lbs	375°F	30 min	2 hrs 15 min
	5 lbs	375°F	30 min	2 hrs 30 min

*Increase roasting time by 15 minutes when chicken is stuffed.

	Weight	Oven Temperature	Internal Temperature	Cooking Time*
Turkey	6 lbs	325°F	180°–185°F	3 hours
	8 lbs	325°F	180°–185°F	3½ hours
	12 lbs	325°F	180°–185°F	4½ hours
	16 lbs	325°F	180°–185°F	5½ hours
	20 lbs	325°F	180°–185°F	6¼ hours

*Unstuffed turkeys require about ½ hour less roasting time.

Baked Short Ribs with Poppy Seed Noodles

Beef short ribs, though not a roast in the usual sense, can also be cooked in the oven, uncovered. A tomatoey barbecue sauce flavors these short ribs. Serve them with noodles.

3 to 4 pounds beef short ribs
  Barbecue Sauce (recipe follows)
1 package (12 oz.) broad egg noodles
  Boiling salted water
1 tablespoon poppy seeds
2 tablespoons butter or margarine
½ cup regular-strength beef broth (homemade or canned)
  Chopped parsley, for garnish

1. Cut short ribs in serving pieces. Arrange on a rack in an uncovered roasting pan. Bake in a 350° oven until browned, 30 to 45 minutes. Pour off and discard fat.

2. Place ribs directly on bottom of roasting pan without rack. Pour on Barbecue Sauce. Continue baking, spooning sauce over meat occasionally, until ribs are tender, around 1 to 1½ hours.

3. About 20 minutes before ribs are done, cook noodles in boiling salted water according to package directions; drain and rinse. Heat poppy seeds in butter in a 2-quart saucepan until bubbly; stir in broth. Bring to boiling and cook for about 5 minutes to reduce slightly. Mix in well-drained noodles.

4. To serve, arrange ribs in center of a warm serving platter; keep warm. Spoon off fat in roasting pan. Add about ½ cup water to sauce in pan; heat and stir. Spoon sauce over meat. Surround with noodles. Sprinkle with chopped parsley.

Makes 6 servings.

Barbecue Sauce: Cook 1 medium onion, chopped, in 1 tablespoon butter or margarine in a 1½-quart saucepan until soft; stir in 1 clove garlic, minced or pressed, ½ teaspoon salt, ¼ teaspoon chili powder, 1 tablespoon brown sugar, 2 tablespoons cider vinegar, 2 teaspoons Worcestershire sauce, ½ cup catsup and 1 cup water. Heat to boiling over medium heat, stirring occasionally.

Above left: Short ribs of beef, not a roast at all, can nonetheless be roasted deliciously in a barbecue sauce to serve with poppy seed-sprinkled noodles.

Right: Any leftover roast beef makes a wonderful hash. It's best if the beef is rare and the potatoes and onions are both cooked slowly until golden-brown.

Herb-Crusted Cross Rib Roast

Other names for the boneless rolled chuck roast specified in this recipe and the one on page 13 are X-rib roast and Diamond Jim roast. (Standard names for specific cuts of meat are beginning to be adopted nationally, but local designations still hang on in many areas.) This rare beef roast is seasoned with herbs and mustard and served with a nippy horseradish sauce.

1 teaspoon *each* dry mustard and coarsely crushed whole black peppers
½ teaspoon *each* crumbled rosemary and summer savory
1 clove garlic, minced or pressed
1 teaspoon olive oil or salad oil
4½ to 5-pound boneless rolled cross rib roast
  Horseradish Sauce (recipe follows)

1. In a small bowl mix dry mustard, black peppers, rosemary, savory, garlic and olive oil into a paste. Press onto outside surfaces of the roast. Place roast, fat side up, on a rack in a shallow roasting pan.

2. Roast, uncovered, in a 325° oven until meat thermometer registers 135° (rare) to 145° (medium-rare to medium), 1½ to 2 hours.

3. Let stand for a few minutes before carving into thin slices. Serve with Horseradish Sauce.

Makes 8 to 10 servings.

Horseradish Sauce: In a chilled bowl combine 1 cup whipping cream, 1 teaspoon sugar, a dash of salt and 1 teaspoon lemon juice; beat with chilled beaters until stiff. Fold in 3 tablespoons prepared horseradish. Chill for 1 to 2 hours to blend flavors. Makes about 2 cups sauce.

Roast Beef Hash with Fried Eggs

Rare leftover roast beef makes a hash that is special, served with dark bread, a cucumber salad and cold beer.

½ cup butter or margarine
2 large onions, finely chopped
½ teaspoon sugar
2 cups cubed cooked potatoes
3 cups rare cooked roast beef, cut in ½-inch cubes
¼ cup regular-strength beef broth (homemade or canned)
1 teaspoon Worcestershire sauce
½ teaspoon salt
⅛ teaspoon pepper
4 to 6 eggs
Chopped parsley, for garnish

1. Heat about 3 tablespoons of the butter in a large frying pan over moderate heat until foamy. Add onions and sugar; cook slowly, stirring occasionally until onions are soft and golden, about 20 minutes.

2. In another large frying pan, melt 3 tablespoons more butter over moderately high heat; add potatoes. Cook until browned on all sides.

3. Remove cooked onions from pan and to it add 1 tablespoon more butter. In it stir beef until it is heated through and lightly browned.

4. To pan with potatoes, add cooked onions and beef; keep warm in a 250° oven. To pan in which onions and beef were cooked, add broth, Worcestershire sauce, salt and pepper; cook over high heat, stirring, until reduced by half. Lightly mix liquid into hash.

5. Serve hash topped with eggs fried in remaining butter to desired doneness. Sprinkle with parsley.

Makes 4 to 6 servings.

Mushroom-Stuffed Meat Loaf

This meat loaf, stuffed with seasoned chopped mushrooms, is special enough for a company meal.

2 tablespoons butter or margarine
¾ pound mushrooms, chopped
1 medium onion, finely chopped
1 teaspoon lemon juice
2 cups soft bread crumbs
½ teaspoon garlic salt
¼ teaspoon crumbled thyme
¼ cup chopped parsley
2 eggs
¼ cup catsup
2 teaspoons prepared mustard
1 teaspoon Worcestershire sauce
1½ teaspoons salt
2 pounds ground beef

1. In a large frying pan, heat butter and cook chopped mushrooms with onion until lightly browned. Remove from heat and lightly mix in lemon juice, then ½ cup of the bread crumbs, garlic salt, thyme and parsley.

2. Beat eggs with catsup, mustard, Worcestershire sauce and salt. Lightly mix in remaining bread crumbs and ground beef.

3. Pat half of the ground beef mixture into a 9 by 5-inch loaf pan. Top with mushroom stuffing. Cover with remaining meat mixture. Bake, uncovered, in a 350° oven for about 1 hour and 15 minutes, until browned. Let stand for a few minutes, remove from pan to slice.

Makes 6 to 8 servings.

Harvest Veal or Turkey Loaf

Use either ground veal or turkey in this golden-flecked meat loaf made with shredded winter squash.

2 cups shredded, peeled banana or Hubbard squash
1½ pounds ground veal or turkey
1 small onion, finely chopped
1 small can (2 oz.) mushroom pieces and stems, drained
1 cup soft bread crumbs
1 teaspoon salt
⅛ teaspoon pepper
¼ teaspoon poultry seasoning
1 cup sour cream

1. Lightly mix squash with ground meat, onion, mushrooms, bread crumbs, seasonings and sour cream.

2. Pat meat mixture into 9 by 5-inch loaf pan. Bake, uncovered, in a 375° oven 1½ hours, until browned.

Makes 6 servings.

Flamed with bourbon, spareribs can be presented elegantly.

Pork

Tangy Marinated Roast Pork Butt

The versatile pork butt roast, a shoulder cut, is juicy and flavorful and often a very good buy. This one is butterflied, the better to absorb the flamboyant flavors of the onion, pimiento and garlic marinade.

    ½ cup cider vinegar
    ¼ cup salad oil
1½ teaspoons salt
    ½ teaspoon crumbled oregano
    ¼ teaspoon pepper
    2 cloves garlic, minced or pressed
    1 large onion, finely chopped
    1 can (4 oz.) pimientos, seeded and chopped
4½ to 5-pound boneless pork butt roast
    Chopped parsley, for garnish

1. In blender or a jar, combine vinegar, oil, salt, oregano, pepper and garlic; whirl or shake until well blended. Add onion and pimientos.

2. Butterfly roast (see illustration), cutting it horizontally through the center, almost to opposite side, then opening it flat. Place meat on a cutting board and score fat side in ½-inch-deep cuts, making about 3-inch squares. Place meat, scored-side up, in a glass baking dish and pour on marinade, spreading onions and pimientos evenly. Cover and refrigerate for 2 to 3 hours.

3. Remove meat, reserving marinade with most of the onion and pimientos.

Place meat, fat side up, on rack in a shallow roasting pan. Spoon on some of the marinade. Roast, uncovered, in a 325° oven, adding marinade occasionally, until meat thermometer registers 170°, about 2 hours.

4. To serve, reheat remaining marinade for sauce and cut meat into squares along scored lines; spoon warm sauce over. Sprinkle with chopped parsley.

Makes 8 to 10 servings.

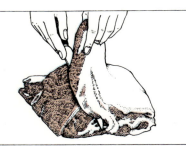

Cut horizontally through center of boneless roast, almost to opposite side.

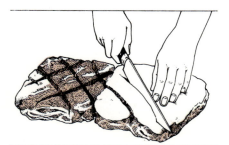

Spread meat flat, then score surface in big squares, the better to absorb flavors of the pimiento marinade.

Cider-Glazed Spareribs Flamed in Bourbon

Because pork spareribs, like short ribs of beef, can be roasted so easily, they are included in this chapter with the more substantial roasts. Cider glazes the ribs as they finish baking. Served flamed in bourbon, they make a spectacular presentation.

    4 pounds spareribs, cut in serving-size pieces
        Garlic salt and pepper
    ½ cup apple cider
    ¼ cup bourbon whiskey

1. Sprinkle spareribs on all sides with garlic salt and pepper. Arrange in a single layer, bone sides down, in a shallow roasting pan or broiler pan. Bake in a 350° oven for 1 hour; pour off all the fat in the pan.

2. Pour cider over spareribs. Replace in oven and continue baking about 30 minutes longer, basting occasionally with pan drippings, until ribs are tender and well browned. Remove to a warm serving platter.

3. Pour off fat in roasting pan. Add bourbon to warm roasting pan, stirring to remove brown bits. Ignite, and spoon, flaming, over spareribs. Cut ribs apart, if you wish.

Makes 4 servings.

Roast Pork with Mustard Potatoes

Try this pork butt as an herb-seasoned rolled roast baked atop thinly sliced potatoes.

    2 teaspoons garlic salt
    ¼ teaspoon seasoned pepper
    ½ teaspoon crumbled summer savory
4½ to 5-pound rolled boneless pork butt roast
    6 medium-size new potatoes (about 2½ lbs.), thinly sliced
    1 medium onion, finely chopped
    ½ cup each chicken broth (canned or homemade) and half-and-half (light cream)
    1 tablespoon Dijon-style mustard

1. Mix garlic salt, seasoned pepper and savory. Rub lightly over outside of pork roast; mix any remaining seasoning mixture with potatoes and onion. Mix broth, cream and mustard until smooth; combine lightly with potatoes. Spread potato mixture in a large, shallow, greased baking dish. Place the seasoned roast, fat side up, in the center of the potatoes.

2. Bake in a 325° oven for 2½ to 3 hours, until meat thermometer registers 170° and potatoes are well browned. Spoon off excess fat before slicing meat.

Makes 6 to 8 servings.

Roast Country-Style Spareribs with Sauerkraut

Dependably moist and meaty, country-style spareribs are delicious baked with zestfully seasoned sauerkraut and served with new potatoes and crusty rye bread.

1 large can (27 oz.) sauerkraut, rinsed and drained
½ teaspoon juniper berries or whole allspice
1 bay leaf
1 medium onion, thinly sliced
4 to 5 pounds country-style spareribs
1 tablespoon *each* kosher or coarse salt and caraway seed
½ teaspoon pepper
½ cup apple cider

1. Mix sauerkraut, juniper berries or allspice, bay leaf and sliced onion. Spread evenly in an ungreased, shallow 2 to 3-quart casserole.

2. Rub spareribs on all sides with a mixture of salt, caraway seed and pepper. Arrange over the sauerkraut, bony sides up, in a single layer. Cover and roast in a 350° oven for 1 hour.

3. Turn spareribs, pour on cider, replace in oven and continue baking, uncovered, for 1 hour and 15 to 30 minutes longer, until spareribs are tender and well browned.

Makes 6 servings.

Glazed Fresh Picnic Shoulder Roast

Also from the pork shoulder is the roast that, when smoked, is known as a picnic. A fresh (unsmoked) picnic is easy to bone and roll for this succulent, mahogany-glazed roast. Serve with a spicy fruit chutney.

5½ to 6-pound bone-in fresh picnic shoulder roast
½ cup *each* soy sauce, honey and water
¼ cup dry red wine
2 tablespoons sugar
½ teaspoon ground ginger
1 teaspoon *each* salt and dry mustard
2 cloves garlic, thinly slivered

1. Remove and discard rind, if any. Bone and tie the roast as shown in the illustrations. Place in a bowl or casserole that is a little larger than the roast.

2. In a small saucepan heat together remaining ingredients, stirring until honey and sugar are dissolved. Cool to room temperature, then pour over roast. Cover and refrigerate 8 hours or overnight, turning several times.

3. Remove meat, reserving marinade, and place, fat side up, on a rack in an open roasting pan. Roast, uncovered,

in a 325° oven until meat thermometer registers 170°, 2 to 2½ hours. During roasting brush occasionally with marinade (any leftover marinade can be stored in refrigerator and reused for chicken, steak or hamburgers). Slice thinly to serve.

Makes 8 to 10 servings.

A fresh picnic shoulder roast usually has but one major bone (if the small hock end is present, cut it off at the joint and save it for soup). The big arm bone goes right down the center; you can see both ends of it. Cut in from one side to expose the bone.

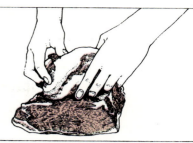

Remove bone and begin rolling the roast.

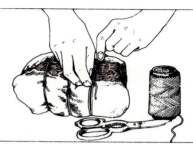

Last, tie the roast firmly at about 2-inch intervals using kitchen string. After marinating, roast on a rack, fat side up. Trim fat before boning and rolling.

Versatile country-style spareribs will be roasted with well-seasoned sauerkraut for a hearty fall or winter supper.

Pinkish-rare roast lamb shoulder with garlic seasoned beans.

Lamb and Veal

If your meat dealer can be induced to bone a lamb shoulder roast, by all means let him. But if you have to bone this economical roast yourself—courage! The process is rather involved, and the first time you do it, you will probably feel like Attila the Hun. However, the second time it will be much easier and neater, and the third time you will scarcely need to glance at the step-by-step illustrations.

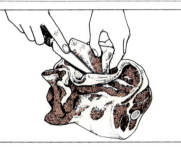

Find long narrow blade bone. Cutting close to bone, cut all the way to joint with arm bone. Cut through joint; lift out blade bone.

Cut under ribs to big middle (chine) bone.

Now cut around arm bone and remove it.

From other side, cut beneath small (feather) bones; lift out entire section.

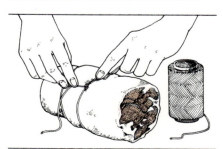

To roll roast, trim excess inside fat; roll lengthwise. Tie at 1-inch intervals.

Rolled Lamb Shoulder with White Beans

4 to 4½-pound lamb shoulder roast, boned
2 cloves garlic, slivered
¼ teaspoon crumbled thyme
　Coarsely ground black pepper
　Cooked White Beans (recipe follows)
　Watercress, for garnish

1. Roll and tie lamb shoulder roast as shown. Cut small gashes in surface of lamb and insert garlic slivers. Sprinkle the meat with thyme and pepper. Place on a rack in a shallow roasting pan. Roast, uncovered, in 325° oven 1¼ to 1½ hours, until meat thermometer registers 140° to 145° for a pink interior color.

2. Carve lamb in ¼-inch-thick slices and accompany with white beans, spooning pan juices over all. Garnish with bouquets of watercress.

Makes 6 servings.

White Beans: In a large kettle bring to boiling 7 cups water and 1 pound dried small white beans (rinsed and drained). Boil vigorously for 2 minutes. Cover, remove from heat and let stand 1 hour. Add 2 teaspoons salt, 1 onion (sliced), 1 stalk celery (chopped), 1 teaspoon crumbled marjoram and ⅛ teaspoon white pepper. Bring to boiling, reduce heat and boil gently, covered, for 1½ to 2 hours, until beans are tender and most of the liquid is absorbed. In a large frying pan sauté 3 cloves garlic, minced or pressed, in 3 tablespoons butter or margarine until garlic begins to brown. Add beans and their liquid and cook, uncovered, stirring occasionally, until thickened but still moist. Taste and add salt, if needed; stir in ¼ cup chopped parsley.

Stuffed Lamb Shoulder Provençale

This roast has a tasty pork and ripe olive stuffing.

½ teaspoon crumbled marjoram
¼ teaspoon *each* crumbled
 rosemary and thyme
1 egg
2 tablespoons milk
1 cup soft French bread crumbs
1 cup ground ham
½ pound ground lean pork
1 clove garlic, minced or pressed
¼ cup chopped ripe olives
 Dash pepper
4¾ to 5-pound lamb shoulder roast,
 boned
 Olive oil

1. Mix marjoram, rosemary and thyme. Beat egg lightly with milk. Mix in bread crumbs, then ground ham and pork, garlic, olives, pepper and ½ teaspoon of the herb mixture.

2. Fill cavity in roast with stuffing mixture; sew edges closed with string or heavy thread. Rub olive oil lightly over surface of meat; sprinkle with remaining herb mixture. Place stuffed roast on a rack in an uncovered roasting pan in a 325° oven.

3. Roast for about 2 hours, until meat thermometer registers 170°. Remove strings; carve meat into ¾-inch slices. Use drippings to make gravy, if you wish. (See page 23.)

Makes about 6 servings.

Spinach-Stuffed Breast of Veal

Although breast of veal is included in this chapter because of its size and dramatic appearance, it is actually cooked covered at least part of the time to keep the meat moist.

 This baked veal breast is frankly Italian with its meaty stuffing of ground beef, spinach and cheese. Accompanied by a salad or green vegetable, it will serve a large group economically.

3 to 3½-pound breast of veal
 Ground Beef and Spinach Stuffing
 (recipe follows)
2 tablespoons olive oil or salad oil
1 cup *each* regular-strength chicken
 broth (canned or homemade) and
 dry white wine

1. When you buy the veal breast, have the meat dealer cut a pocket for the stuffing.

2. Fill the pocket with the stuffing, fastening the open end with small metal

skewers. Place the meat in a large roasting pan. Brush with oil. Pour on ¾ cup *each* of the broth and wine. Cover with foil and bake in a 325° oven for 2 hours, until meat is very tender. Increase oven temperature to 350° and continue baking, uncovered, for 25 to 30 minutes longer, brushing occasionally with pan drippings, to brown meat attractively. Remove meat to a warm platter and keep it warm.

3. Loosen pan drippings with remaining ¼ cup *each* broth and wine, stirring over high heat until liquid is reduced by about a third. Serve the sauce separately. To carve, cut between the rib bones.

Makes 6 to 8 servings.

Ground Beef and Spinach Stuffing: Crumble ½ pound ground beef and brown it in its own drippings in a large frying pan; mix in 1 medium onion (chopped), 1 clove garlic (minced or pressed) and 1 small can (2 oz.) mushroom pieces and stems, well drained. Cook, stirring occasionally, until onion is soft and begins to brown. Remove from heat and mix in 1 package (9 or 10 oz.) frozen chopped spinach, thawed and squeezed dry. Add ½ cup soft bread crumbs, 1 cup shredded Monterey jack cheese, 1 egg (slightly beaten), ½ teaspoon *each* salt and basil and ⅛ teaspoon seasoned pepper; mix lightly.

Poultry

Sausage-Stuffed Roast Chicken

You can prepare the savory stuffing for this roast chicken ahead of time, if you wish, and refrigerate it. But to be on the safe side, wait until cooking time to stuff the bird.

5-pound roasting chicken
 Sausage Stuffing (recipe follows)
3 slices bacon
1 cup chicken broth (*or* ½ cup *each*
 chicken broth and dry white wine)

1. Rinse chicken with running cool water, inside and out, and pat dry with paper towel. Reserve liver for stuffing; save remaining giblets to make broth for later dish. Fill breast and body cavities with stuffing; skewer closed. Place any extra stuffing in a buttered, covered casserole. Drape bacon slices over the breast and insert meat thermometer in thickest part of breast. Place the chicken on a rack in a shallow pan.

2. Roast chicken, uncovered, in a 325° oven (thermometer registers 175°) or until leg moves freely, 1½ to 2 hours. Bake extra stuffing during last 30 minutes. Remove chicken to a carving platter and keep warm.

3. Skim off fat from roasting pan. Add broth (or combined broth and wine) to pan and cook over direct heat, stirring constantly, to loosen brown drippings and reduce liquid by about a third. Serve sauce with slices of the carved chicken.

Makes 6 servings.

Sausage Stuffing: Crumble 1 pound bulk pork sausage into a large frying pan and begin browning it over moderately high heat. Add 1 onion (finely chopped), the liver from the chicken (coarsely chopped) and 1 clove garlic (minced or pressed: optional). Continue cooking until sausage is browned and onion is soft. Remove from heat. Spoon off and discard fat. Add 3 cups cubed French bread, ½ cup shredded Parmesan cheese and ¼ cup chopped parsley. Then lightly mix in about ⅓ cup chicken broth, just enough to moisten. Makes about 5 cups.

Flaming Cornish Hens on a Spit

When frozen Rock Cornish game hens are advertised at a special price, take advantage of their economy for this lavish treatment. It makes a splendid dinner for two. Cooked on a rotisserie, the little birds are served flaming in your choice of brandy, whiskey or orange liqueur.

2 Rock Cornish game hens (24 oz.
 ***each*)**
2 tablespoons butter or margarine
1 teaspoon lemon juice
½ teaspoon grated orange rind
⅛ teaspoon whole white or black
 peppers, crushed
 Dash nutmeg
¼ cup brandy, bourbon, Scotch or
 orange-flavored liqueur (such as
 Grand Marnier or Cointreau)

1. Arrange Cornish hens on a spit in oven or on a portable electric rotisserie. Heat together butter, lemon juice, orange rind, crushed peppers and nutmeg until bubbling.

2. Spit-roast hens, brushing occasionally with butter mixture, until skin is crisp and well browned, 1½ to 2 hours. Remove spit with Cornish hens to a warm heatproof (not wooden) platter; keep warm.

3. In a small long-handled pan, heat brandy, whiskey or liqueur just until lukewarm (overheating will prevent flaming). Ignite and pour over chickens, spooning on the flaming liquid until flames are exhausted. Serve whole chicken with juices spooned over, with thick slices of warm French bread to mop up juices. Eat with your fingers, if you like.

Makes 2 servings.

Honey-Glazed Baked Chicken Quarters

Baked chicken quarters with a sweet-and-sour glaze are another simple oven dish.

3 to 3½-pound chicken, quartered (see page 9)
⅓ cup flour
1 teaspoon garlic salt
Dash pepper
6 tablespoons butter or margarine
¼ cup honey
3 tablespoons lemon juice
2 tablespoons soy sauce
Dash ground ginger

1. Coat chicken quarters thoroughly with a mixture of flour, garlic salt and pepper. As oven preheats to 350°, melt 2 tablespoons of the butter in a shallow baking dish just large enough to hold the chicken in a single layer. Arrange chicken, skin side down, in melted butter. Bake, uncovered, 30 minutes.

2. Meanwhile, melt remaining 4 tablespoons butter with honey, lemon juice, soy sauce and ginger. When chicken has baked 30 minutes, turn and evenly pour on butter mixture. Continue baking, brushing occasionally with sauce, for about 30 to 40 minutes longer, until chicken is tender and richly browned.

Makes 4 servings.

Piquant Roast Chicken Halves

Look for small chickens—two and a half pounds or less—to use in this recipe. Though low in calories, these roast chickens have a lot of flavor.

2 small (about 2½ lbs. *each*) chickens, halved (see page 9)
2 tablespoons salad oil
3 tablespoons lemon juice
2 teaspoons salt
1 teaspoon *each* tarragon and paprika
½ teaspoon Tabasco sauce

1. Place chicken halves, skin side down, in a shallow nonstick baking pan. In a jar or small blender container, shake or whirl together remaining ingredients. Brush about half of the mixture generously over chicken.

2. Bake in a 375° oven for about 1 hour. Turn chicken after the first 30 minutes and brush several times during baking with remaining seasonings, until chicken is tender and nicely browned.

Makes 4 servings.

Quartered chicken is baked to a rich brown with a glaze of honey, lemon juice, soy sauce and ginger.

Roast Turkey with Cornbread Dressing

Festively stuffed with cornbread and sausage, turkey deserves the place of honor it occupies on holiday dinner tables. And it's often even more economical when presented for a special occasion outside the holiday season.

1 pound bulk pork sausage
2 onions, finely chopped
1 cup chopped celery
5 cups crumbled cornbread (recipe follows)
3 cups cubed, day-old French bread
½ teaspoon salt
½ cup chopped parsley
⅓ to ½ cup turkey or chicken broth (homemade or canned)
12 to 15-pound turkey, thawed, rinsed and patted dry
2 to 3 tablespoons soft butter or margarine

1. Crumble pork sausage into a large frying pan. Cook, stirring, until browned. Pour off all but about 3 tablespoons of the drippings. Add onions and celery and continue cooking, stirring occasionally, until vegetables are tender. In a large bowl combine cornbread and French bread. Lightly stir in sausage mixture, salt and parsley. Gradually add broth, stirring just until stuffing is moistened.

2. Stuff the dressing lightly into the breast and body cavities; skewer or sew closed. Tie legs together, if you wish. Place turkey on a rack in a shallow pan. Rub all over with butter. Insert thermometer in thick part of thigh.

3. Roast, uncovered, in a 325° oven until thermometer registers 180° to 185° and drumstick moves easily, 2½ to 3½ hours. During roasting, baste several times with pan drippings. Let turkey stand on warmed platter, covered loosely with foil, for about 15 minutes before carving.

4. Meanwhile, make gravy using pan drippings, if you wish.

Makes 12 to 15 servings.

Cornbread: Into a mixing bowl sift together 1 cup unsifted all-purpose flour, ¼ cup sugar, 2 teaspoons baking powder, ¾ teaspoon salt and ½ teaspoon baking soda. Mix in 1 cup yellow cornmeal. Make a well in center, and into it place 1 egg, 1 cup buttermilk or sour milk and 2 tablespoons salad oil. Stir together quickly, just enough to moisten dry ingredients. Spread in a greased 8-inch-square pan. Bake in a 425° oven for 15 to 20 minutes until top is lightly browned and a wooden pick inserted near center comes out clean. Cool before crumbling for the dressing. Remaining cornbread can be frozen, if you wish.

Perfect Gravy
How to make it.

For many people a beef roast or turkey are incomplete without rich brown gravy. Here are some ideas for making your gravy smooth and flavorful.

Think of gravy as a thickened sauce, then follow the same procedure as when you make a white sauce. After removing the meat from the roasting pan, pour or spoon off and measure the fat. For each cup of gravy, measure 1 to 2 tablespoons of fat into a saucepan (discard the rest).

Loosen the drippings in the pan with liquid—beef or chicken broth, if you have it, water, or red or white wine (or a combination of broth or water and wine). Heat and stir to loosen brown bits, and pour the liquid into a measuring cup; pour it through a sieve if there are large undissolved bits. Don't add too much liquid, or the flavor will be weak.

For each cup of liquid, measure 1 to 2 tablespoons flour. Stir the flour into the fat in the saucepan and heat until bubbly. Remove from heat. Using a wire whisk, gradually stir in the liquid. Return to heat and cook, stirring constantly, until thickened and boiling. Boil gently, stirring, 3 to 5 minutes longer. Salt to taste.

If you prefer a creamy gravy for pork or chicken, use about half milk for the liquid, with broth or water.

Thirty-Minute Meats

The cook in a hurry need not fall back on the costliest cuts. Thrifty meats can be broiled, barbecued, sautéed or stir-fried quickly.

People often assume that cooking inexpensive meats takes forever. While some of the less costly cuts do clearly benefit by long slow cooking (you'll find them in the next two chapters), many can be deliciously prepared by the time-conscious cook in half an hour or less. Here are some of the methods of quick cooking.

Broiling

Many of the most elegant dishes restaurants serve are broiled—and not all of them start with fancy meats. With marinades, handsome presentation and judicious use of some of the thrifty cuts of meat and poultry you have already learned to recognize as good values, you can do it too.

Broiled Steak Satay with Pineapple

Marinating top round in soy sauce with sherry, garlic and onions helps to tenderize and flavor this lean meat. Strips of the steak are threaded onto skewers and broiled with wedges of pineapple, then sprinkled with ground sesame seeds in the Indonesian style. The steak skewers and fruit are good with rice and a stir-fried green vegetable, such as edible-pod peas.

1½ to 2 pounds top round steak,
  ¾ inch thick
⅓ cup soy sauce
3 tablespoons dry sherry
2 tablespoons salad oil
1 small onion, finely chopped
3 cloves garlic, minced or pressed
¼ cup orange marmalade
⅛ teaspoon cayenne
1 small pineapple (about 2 lbs.)
2 tablespoons sesame seeds,
  toasted and ground (directions
  follow)
  Plain unflavored yogurt
  Lime or lemon wedges

Chicken legs are barbecued with a mustard-herb marinade. See the recipe, page 29, plus accompanying menu ideas.

Versatile top round is tenderly marinated, threaded on skewers, served with fresh pineapple, Chinese peas.

1. Cut steak into 6 long strips, each about ¾ inch wide. For marinade, mix soy sauce, sherry, oil, onion and garlic. Place steak strips in bowl with marinade. Cover and refrigerate 1 to 2 hours.

2. Shortly before serving, whirl marmalade in blender with about 2 tablespoons of the marinade and cayenne. Peel pineapple, quarter and remove core; cut in about 12 long wedges. Remove steak from marinade and thread strips on 6 individual metal or bamboo skewers, weaving skewer in and out of meat lengthwise to give a serpentine effect. Arrange skewers on rack of a broiler pan. Broil 3 to 4 inches from heat until well browned on first side, 4 to 5 minutes.

3. Turn skewers, and around them arrange pineapple wedges; brush generously with marmalade mixture. Continue broiling until meat is browned to taste and pineapple is lightly browned, turning pineapple once and brushing again with marmalade mixture.

4. Sprinkle meat with ground toasted sesame seeds. Serve with hot broiled

pineapple, accompanied by unflavored yogurt and lime wedges to add at the table to taste.

Makes 6 servings.

To toast and grind sesame seeds: Spread 2 tablespoons sesame seeds in a shallow pan and bake in a 350° oven until lightly browned, 8 to 10 minutes; cool slightly. Whirl in small blender jar, or crush in a mortar, until powdery.

Mixed Grill en Brochette

A mixed grill usually combines several tender loin cuts of beef, lamb and pork—a tiny fillet steak, a loin chop—and variety meats such as liver or kidney. Here is a less expensive version, attractively broiled on long skewers.

You can have the skewered meats prepared ahead and refrigerated, ready to place in the broiler about 20 minutes before dinner. A colorful accompaniment is crumb and cheese-topped tomato halves. For a vegetable you might choose tender young Brussels sprouts.

Thrifty Mixed Grill en Brochette.

1 pound top round, about 1 inch thick
Unseasoned powdered meat tenderizer
4 slices bacon
8 chicken livers
1 egg
¼ cup fine dry bread crumbs
1 clove garlic, minced or pressed
1 teaspoon salt
¼ teaspoon crumbled oregano
1 pound ground lamb
¼ cup finely chopped parsley
Broiled Tomatoes (recipe follows)

1. Cut round steak into 1-inch cubes; sprinkle with tenderizer on all sides according to label directions; let stand while preparing remaining meats.

2. Cut bacon slices in halves crosswise; cook until bacon is limp and has released most of its fat, but remove from heat before bacon begins to brown; drain. Wrap a partially cooked bacon strip around each chicken liver; set aside.

3. Beat egg slightly; mix in bread crumbs, garlic, salt and oregano, then lightly combine with ground lamb and parsley. Shape into 1-inch balls.

4. On 8 long skewers alternate beef cubes and meatballs with a bacon-wrapped chicken liver in the center of each skewer. Arrange skewers on a rack in a broiler pan. Broil, about 6 inches from heat source, until nicely browned, about 10 minutes for each side, turning once. After turning, arrange tomatoes around the meat and broil them until they are heated through and lightly browned.

Makes 8 servings.

Broiled Tomatoes: Cut 4 small ripe tomatoes in halves crosswise. Sprinkle with salt and pepper. Lightly mix ½ cup soft bread crumbs, ½ teaspoon onion salt, 2 tablespoons melted butter or margarine, 1 tablespoon finely chopped parsley and ¼ cup shredded Monterey jack cheese. Spoon mixture over the cut sides of the tomatoes. Broil as directed above.

Marinated London Broil

One of the confusing things about buying meat is that some retailers label certain cuts with names that really identify a method of cooking, rather than the part of the animal from which the cut has come. A good example is London broil. Traditionally, London broil has been prepared with flank steak. Yet the cut of beef labeled "London broil" in a supermarket meat case is usually not flank steak but top round, cut from the most tender part of the round next to the sirloin. From very high quality beef, this can be broiled or barbecued as is. However, you can produce a delicious London broil using a more modest cut of top round if you marinate it first to tenderize and flavor it. Broil it just to the rare stage, then cut the meat in thin slices diagonally across the grain.

1½ to 2 pounds first-cut top round, about 1 inch thick
¼ cup *each* salad oil and dry red wine
1 tablespoon Worcestershire sauce
1 teaspoon Dijon-style mustard
2 cloves garlic, minced or pressed
½ teaspoon salt
¼ teaspoon *each* sugar and crumbled rosemary
1 bay leaf
Seasoned pepper
Chopped parsley, for garnish

1. Place meat in a shallow dish. In a covered jar or blender container, shake or whirl together oil, wine, Worcestershire sauce, mustard, garlic, salt, sugar and rosemary until well combined. Pour over meat, turning to coat well. Place bay leaf in marinade. Cover and refrigerate, turning occasionally, at least 8 to 10 hours.

2. Remove meat from marinade, reserving marinade. Place on a rack in a broiling pan. Sprinkle with pepper. Broil, about 6 inches from heat, until well browned on each side (allow about 10 minutes per side for rare), brushing occasionally with marinade.

3. Place on a wooden board and carve in thin diagonal slices. (See illustration below.) Sprinkle with chopped parsley.

Makes 6 to 8 servings.

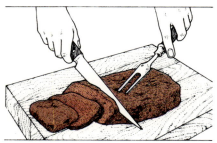

Thinly slice flavorful thick cut of top round on diagonal for tenderness.

Giant Stuffed Hamburger Steaks with Tangy Sauce

Filling plump hamburgers with a creamy, brandied blue cheese butter gives them a special flavor, as does a tangy cold sauce spiked with horseradish. Accompany the hamburger steaks with crisp raw vegetables to dip into the sauce, warm French bread and a red wine such as Beaujolais or a California Zinfandel.

1 medium onion, chopped
3 tablespoons butter or margarine
2 cloves garlic, minced or pressed
2 eggs
2 pounds ground beef
2 tablespoons chopped parsley
1 teaspoon salt
⅛ teaspoon pepper
¼ cup crumbled blue cheese
1 tablespoon brandy
Tangy Sauce (recipe follows)

1. In a small frying pan cook onion in 1 tablespoon of the butter until soft but not browned. Mix in garlic; remove from heat. Beat eggs in a large bowl. Mix in onion mixture, ground beef, parsley, salt and pepper. Shape into 8 flat oval patties.

2. In a small bowl mix blue cheese, remaining 2 tablespoons butter and brandy until creamy and well combined. Place a quarter of the blue cheese mixture in center of each of 4 of the ground beef patties. Top with remaining patties; press edges together to seal.

3. Arrange stuffed hamburgers on rack in a broiler pan. Broil about 4 inches from heat until well browned on both sides, a total of 12 to 15 minutes. Serve with the Tangy Sauce to spoon over each hamburger to taste.

Makes 4 servings.

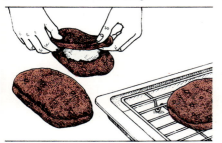

Top four of the large oval ground beef patties with blue cheese filling.

Cover with remaining patties. Press edges together to seal before broiling.

Tangy Sauce: Mix together ¼ cup *each* chili sauce and mayonnaise, ½ cup catsup, 1½ teaspoons *each* dry mustard and red wine vinegar, 1 teaspoon Worcestershire sauce, a dash of Tabasco sauce, ¼ teaspoon ground ginger and 1 tablespoon *each* pineapple juice and horseradish.

Makes about 1¼ cups.

Swiss-Style Skewered Liver and Bacon

Liver and bacon are a combination enjoyed in many parts of the world, including Zurich, where this dish is traditional. There it is usually served with *rösti* (the delicious potatoes that can be likened to very lovingly prepared hash browns). Add fresh green beans.

10 to 12 slices bacon, cut in half crosswise
1 pound young beef liver, sliced
White pepper
½ teaspoon ground sage
Chopped parsley, for garnish

1. Partially cook bacon until limp and beginning to brown; drain on paper towels.

2. Cut liver into strips 1 inch wide and about 2 inches long. Sprinkle lightly with pepper, then with sage. Wrap each liver strip in a partially cooked bacon strip. Thread on 8-inch bamboo skewers, about 3 to a skewer, to hold bacon in place.

3. Arrange skewers on a rack in a broiler pan. Broil, 3 to 4 inches from heat, until bacon is well browned on both sides, turning once (liver should be slightly pink in the center). Serve sprinkled with parsley.

Makes 3 to 4 servings.

Russian Marinated Lamb on Skewers

The piquant, magenta juice of autumn pomegranates is used to marinate lamb in many Russian recipes. Serve the skewered lamb with a rice pilaf and lightly sautéed zucchini. See page 20 for step-by-step directions for boning a lamb shoulder roast to cube.

½ cup fresh pomegranate juice
2 tablespoons lemon juice
1 small onion, finely chopped
2 tablespoons salad oil
1 clove garlic, minced or pressed
½ teaspoon salt
Dash pepper
2 pounds cubed boneless lean lamb shoulder or leg
2 green onions, thinly sliced (use part of tops), for garnish
Lemon wedges and parsley sprigs

1. Mix pomegranate and lemon juices, chopped onion, oil, garlic, salt and pepper in a shallow bowl. Stir in cubed lamb. Cover and refrigerate for 4 to 5 hours or overnight.

2. Drain meat and divide it among 6 skewers. Broil, about 4 inches from heat source, turning once, until well browned on both sides, 8 to 10 minutes. Serve immediately, sprinkled with green onions and garnished with lemon and parsley.

Makes 6 servings.

Fruited Chicken en Brochette

Generous morsels of boneless chicken breast, marinated in spices, wine and yogurt, then skewered with onion and apricots, make a delicious and unusual entrée. A rice pilaf is a pleasant accompaniment with a green vegetable, such as peas or asparagus.

3 whole chicken breasts (6 halves, about 3 lbs.), boned and skinned (see page 9)
½ cup plain unflavored yogurt
¼ cup dry white wine
½ teaspoon cinnamon
¼ teaspoon curry powder
⅛ teaspoon cardamom
½ cup dried apricots
½ cup water
2 tablespoons brown sugar
1 tablespoon lemon juice
½ medium onion, separated into layers and cut in 1-inch squares
Sliced green onions (use part of tops), for garnish
Lemon wedges

1. Cut boned chicken into bite-size squares and place in a shallow glass bowl. Blend yogurt, wine, cinnamon, curry powder and cardamom until smooth and pour over chicken; stir to coat chicken well with marinade. Cover and refrigerate 2 to 4 hours.

2. Meanwhile, place apricots in a small pan with water, brown sugar and lemon juice. Bring to a gentle boil and simmer, uncovered, until apricots are just tender, about 10 minutes. Drain.

3. Remove chicken pieces from marinade and thread onto 6 metal skewers, alternating with onion squares and apricots. Place on a rack in a broiling pan about 6 inches from heat; broil until chicken is cooked in the thickest part (test with a small sharp knife) and lightly browned —10 to 12 minutes per side. Sprinkle with green onions. Serve with lemon to squeeze over chicken.

Makes 6 servings.

Wearing gloves to protect your hands from purple stains, ream fresh pomegranates to make the marinade for Russian boneless lamb cubes on skewers.

Barbecuing

The flavor of meat cooked over charcoal is incomparable. Meats and poultry that can be broiled can also be cooked on your charcoal, gas or electric grill. The following recipes are especially well suited to the barbecue.

Barbecued Chicken Picnic

Set up a barbecue on the patio, in the park or at the beach for this festive picnic featuring barbecued chicken. When you cut a whole chicken into quarters, save the meaty leg and thigh portions to barbecue with this mustard-and-herb marinade.

**Mustard-Barbecued Chicken Legs
Garden Potato Salad
Sliced Tomatoes
Garlic Bread
Orange Chiffon Cake with
Strawberries and Cream
Jug Chablis   Milk   Coffee**

Garden Potato Salad

4 **medium boiling potatoes
  Boiling salted water**
1 **clove garlic**
2 **tablespoons salad oil**
¼ **cup tarragon wine vinegar**
1 **teaspoon** *each* **salt and sugar**
½ **teaspoon dill weed**
3 **hard-cooked eggs**
3 **green onions, sliced**
3 **large radishes, sliced**
1 **small green pepper, quartered,
  seeded and thinly sliced**
¼ **cup sliced ripe olives**
⅓ **cup mayonnaise
  Chopped parsley, for garnish**

1. Cook unpeeled potatoes in boiling salted water just until tender, about 35 minutes. While potatoes are cooking, split garlic and place it in a jar with oil; let stand for 10 minutes. Remove and discard garlic. To oil add vinegar, salt, sugar and dill weed; shake well to blend. Drain potatoes; peel while warm and cut into ½-inch cubes (you should have about 4 cups). Pour dressing over warm potatoes. Cover and chill for several hours or overnight.

2. To serve, slice 2 of the eggs. Add to potatoes with green onions, radishes, green pepper, ripe olives and mayonnaise. Mix lightly. Garnish with remaining egg, sliced, and parsley.

Makes 4 servings.

An elegant patio picnic supper for four includes mustard-barbecued chicken with lively dill-flavored potato salad, warm garlic bread and chiffon cake with berries.

Mustard-Barbecued Chicken Legs

2 **tablespoons Dijon-style mustard**
1 **tablespoon dry white wine**
¼ **teaspoon** *each* **crumbled basil,
  oregano, rosemary and thyme**
1 **clove garlic, minced or pressed**
4 **whole chicken legs (thighs
  attached)**

1. In a small bowl mix mustard, wine, herbs and garlic until well combined. Spread the mustard mixture evenly over all sides of chicken. Cover and refrigerate about 3 hours.

2. Arrange chicken on a barbecue grill about 6 inches above glowing coals. Grill chicken legs until well browned on both sides, turning once, about 45 minutes in all (meat near the thigh bones should no longer be pink or run with pink juices when tested with the point of a small, sharp knife).

Makes 4 servings.

Orange Chiffon Cake with Strawberries and Cream

2¼ **cups sifted cake flour**
1½ **cups sugar**
  3 **teaspoons baking powder**
  1 **teaspoon salt**
  ½ **cup salad oil**
  5 **egg yolks**
  2 **oranges
    Water**
  1 **cup egg whites (whites of about
    8 eggs)**
  ½ **teaspoon cream of tartar
    Whipped cream
    Strawberries**

1. Sift flour, sugar, baking powder and salt into a medium-sized mixing bowl. Make a well in the center and into it place, in order: oil, egg yolks and the grated rind of the 2 oranges. Squeeze and strain orange juice, measure and add water (if needed) to make ¾ cup. Add to egg yolk mixture. Beat until smooth.

2. In a large bowl, beat egg whites and cream of tartar until very stiff peaks form. Gradually pour egg yolk mixture over egg whites, folding gently until the two mixtures are incorporated.

3. Pour batter into an *ungreased* 10-inch tube pan. Bake in a 325° oven for 1 hour to 1 hour and 10 minutes, until long bamboo skewer inserted in thickest part comes out clean. Suspend pan on a funnel or bottle to cool completely. With a thin spatula, gently loosen sides and bottom of cake; invert it onto a serving plate.

4. To serve, top with whipped cream and strawberries.

Makes 8 to 10 servings.

Lemon-Barbecued Lamb Shoulder Chops

The Mediterranean flavor of a spicy marinade with lemon, garlic and oregano enhances economical lamb shoulder chops.

4 **round-bone lamb shoulder chops,
  about ¾ inch thick (about 2 lbs.)**
3 **tablespoons** *each* **olive oil or
  salad oil and lemon juice**
½ **teaspoon** *each* **salt, paprika and
  crumbled oregano**
2 **cloves garlic, minced or pressed**
¼ **teaspoon** *each* **sugar and whole
  black peppers, coarsely crushed**
1 **teaspoon grated lemon rind**
1 **bay leaf**

1. Trim any excess fat from lamb chops. Arrange in a single layer in a shallow baking dish.

2. In a jar or small blender container shake or whirl together oil, lemon juice, salt, paprika, oregano, garlic and sugar until well combined. Mix in black peppers, lemon rind and bay leaf; pour over lamb chops. Cover and refrigerate 2 to 4 hours, turning at least once.

3. Remove chops from marinade, reserving marinade. Grill about 6 inches above glowing coals, brushing occasionally with marinade, until well browned, about 5 minutes per side.

Makes 4 servings.

Barbecued Pork Buns

For a quick family barbecue meal, slice pork butt thinly, marinate it in a savory tomato sauce, then grill the slices quickly to serve in the sauce on toasted sesame rolls. The sandwiches are good with potato chips and salad or corn-on-the-cob.

1 **pound boneless pork butt, fat
  trimmed
  Tomato Barbecue Sauce (see
  page 31)**
4 **hamburger buns with sesame
  seeds
  Dill pickle slices**

1. Freeze meat partially, then cut across the grain into large, thin slices. Place in a shallow bowl and lightly mix with sauce; cover and refrigerate 2 to 3 hours or longer.

2. Remove meat from sauce. Place on grill above glowing coals, and cook, turning with tongs as the meat browns, cooking just until nicely browned on both sides. As meat cooks, remove to a covered dish and keep warm.

3. Reheat sauce. Toast split hamburger buns on grill. Make sandwiches by filling toasted buns with cooked meat, spooning warm sauce over, and topping with pickles.

Makes 4 servings.

Mexican Steak Barbecue

Using that thick first cut of the top round (as in London Broil) tenderized by an assertive chile-garlic-tequila marinade, you can produce a rare, juicy steak reminiscent of Mexico's *carne asada*. With sangria or beer, a baked tomato-rice casserole and re-fried beans topped with sharp cheese, this dish really invites a party.

**Mexican-Barbecued Top Round
Tomato Rice Casserole
Refried Beans with Cheese
Corn Chips   Hot Sauce
Fresh Fruit   Sugar Cookies
Easy Sangria or Beer**

Refried Beans with Cheese

1 large onion, chopped
3 tablespoons lard, bacon drippings
   or salad oil
1 large can (30 oz.) refried beans
1 clove garlic, minced or pressed
2 teaspoons chili powder
1 cup shredded Cheddar cheese

1. In a heavy frying pan cook onion in heated lard, drippings or oil, stirring until lightly browned. Mix in beans, garlic and chili powder.

2. Cook over medium heat, stirring occasionally, until fat is absorbed and beans are heated through, about 5 minutes. Mix in ½ cup of the cheese until melted; serve from frying pan, topped with remaining cheese.

Makes 6 servings.

Tomato Rice Casserole

1½ cups long grain rice
   3 tablespoons salad oil
   1 large onion, finely chopped
   1 clove garlic, minced or pressed
   1 large can (15 oz.) tomato sauce
1½ cups regular-strength chicken
      broth, homemade or canned
   ¾ teaspoon *each* salt and cumin
   ⅛ teaspoon cayenne
   ¾ cup ripe olive wedges
   2 cups shredded Monterey jack
      cheese

1. In a large deep saucepan stir rice to coat it with heated oil; stir in onion and garlic and cook until onion browns lightly. Mix in tomato sauce, broth,

salt, cumin and cayenne. Bring to boiling, reduce heat and cover tightly. Cook until rice is almost tender, about 20 minutes.

2. Mix in olive wedges and 1 cup of the cheese. Turn into a greased 1½ to 2-quart casserole. Sprinkle with remaining cheese. Bake, uncovered, in a 375° oven until cheese is melted and lightly browned, about 15 minutes.

Makes 6 to 8 servings.

Mexican Barbecued Top Round

1½ to 2 pounds first-cut top round,
      about 1 inch thick
   ¼ cup salad oil
   3 tablespoons tequila
   1 small dried hot chile pepper,
      crushed
   1 tablespoon chili powder
   1 teaspoon salt
   ¼ teaspoon crumbled oregano
   2 cloves garlic, minced or pressed
   ¼ cup *each* slivered red and
      green bell peppers
      and mild red onion
      Radish roses, for garnish

1. Place meat in a shallow glass dish. In a covered jar or small blender container shake or whirl together oil, tequila, dried chile, chili powder, salt, oregano and garlic. Pour over meat. Cover and refrigerate, turning occasionally, at least 8 to 10 hours.

2. Remove meat from marinade, reserving marinade. Place on grill about 6 inches above glowing coals. Barbecue, brushing occasionally with marinade, until well browned on each side, 10 minutes per side for rare steak.

3. Place on a wooden board and carve in thin, slightly diagonal slices. Top with mixture of red and green bell peppers and onion. Garnish with radishes.

Makes 6 to 8 servings.

Easy Sangria

1 large can (12 oz.) frozen limeade
      concentrate, thawed
1 quart dry red wine
      Orange, lemon, lime and straw-
      berry slices
1 quart chilled club soda

1. In a 10 to 12-cup pitcher, stir together limeade concentrate and wine. Mix in fruit slices to taste. Cover and chill for 3 to 4 hours.

2. To serve, mix in club soda. Add ice and garnish with additional sliced fruit, if you wish.

Makes 6 to 8 servings.

Slice barbecued top round thinly to serve with Mexican accompaniments —a rice casserole, beans, red wine punch, fresh fruit and your favorite sugar cookies.

Brochettes of pork and red peppers grill with zucchini slices.

Skewered Pork and Red Peppers

A marinade of wine, lemon and herbs for the pork also makes a flavorful baste for big, thick, diagonal slices of zucchini. Grill the zucchini over the charcoal fire with these colorful brochettes of pork, peppers and onions.

1½ to 2 pounds lean boneless pork butt, cut in 1-inch cubes
½ cup dry white wine
   Juice of 1 lemon
2 tablespoons olive oil or salad oil
1 teaspoon *each* salt and paprika
¼ teaspoon *each* pepper and crumbled rosemary
1 large onion
1 large red bell pepper, halved and seeded

1. Place pork cubes in a shallow bowl. Shake or whirl together in blender wine, lemon juice, oil, salt, paprika, pepper and rosemary. Cut onion in half; chop half finely and add to pork (reserve remaining half). Pour marinade over pork. Cover and refrigerate 8 to 10 hours or overnight.

2. Remove pork from bowl, reserving marinade. Cut remaining half onion in wedges, then separate into layers and cut into squares. Cut red pepper into 1-inch squares. Alternate pork cubes on 4 to 6 skewers with onion and red pepper squares.

3. Grill skewered pork about 6 inches above glowing coals, brushing occasionally with reserved marinade, until nicely browned on each side, 8 to 10 minutes per side.

Makes 4 to 6 servings.

Three Versatile Marinades for Barbecued Meats

Marinating meat and poultry can make a big difference in its flavor and tenderness when barbecued. The three following marinades are good examples of different styles.

For marinating use a container that snugly holds the meat in a single layer. A glass or stainless steel bowl or casserole is a good choice, as it won't be affected by acid ingredients. Cover the marinating meat with plastic wrap or the casserole cover and refrigerate it for several hours or as long as overnight for maximum flavor.

Any leftover marinade can be stored in a covered jar in the refrigerator for another use up to a month. (The teriyaki marinade keeps for several months).

Tomato Barbecue Sauce

1 medium onion, finely chopped
1 tablespoon salad oil
1 large clove garlic, minced or pressed
½ teaspoon *each* salt and chili powder
¼ teaspoon dry mustard
2 tablespoons brown sugar
3 tablespoons cider vinegar
1 tablespoon Worcestershire sauce
¾ cup *each* catsup and dry red wine

1. Cook onion in oil in a 1½ to 2-quart saucepan until soft but not browned; stir in garlic, salt, chili powder, dry mustard, brown sugar, vinegar, Worcestershire sauce, catsup and wine. Stir until sugar dissolves and mixture begins to boil; simmer for 3 to 5 minutes, then remove from heat.

2. Cool before using as a marinade for uncooked meat and poultry such as pork, beef or chicken. Or brush, warm, over hamburgers or frankfurters as they cook on grill. Warm sauce can also be used for reheating sliced cooked beef, pork or chicken (this recipe is used in Barbecued Pork Buns, page 29).

Makes about 2 cups.

Teriyaki Marinade

½ cup soy sauce
3 tablespoons sugar
2 teaspoons grated fresh ginger, *or* ½ teaspoon ground ginger
1 clove garlic, minced or pressed
2 tablespoons dry sherry

1. In a bowl or tightly covered jar, mix or shake all ingredients well, until sugar is dissolved.

2. Use as a marinade for beef steaks or chicken pieces, quarters or halves. Brush with marinade while cooking.

Makes about ¾ cup.

Mustard and Herb Marinade

⅓ cup salad oil
¼ cup dry white wine
1 tablespoon *each* red wine vinegar and lemon juice
1 large clove garlic, minced or pressed
1½ tablespoons Dijon-style mustard
¼ teaspoon *each* salt and sugar
⅛ teaspoon *each* thyme, oregano, summer savory and tarragon
   Dash white pepper

1. Combine all ingredients in blender container; whirl until smooth.

2. Use as a marinade for lamb or chicken.

Makes a little less than 1 cup.

Versatile barbecue marinades (clockwise from top left) include gingery teriyaki, mustard-herb and a tangy tomato sauce.

Top-of-the-Range Cooking

Several kinds of very speedy meat cooking can be done on your range top or in an electric frying pan—or even over a hot plate! *Pan broiling* is done in a frying pan over moderately high heat, using little if any cooking fat. *Pan frying or sautéeing* is another means of quick skillet cooking, using more fat than pan broiling. And *stir-frying* is familiar to all devotées of Chinese cooking (see page 43).

When you are preparing a meat dish using any of these quick-cooking techniques, it is a good idea to have all your ingredients peeled, chopped, measured and ready to use. Success depends on putting the various elements together swiftly and smoothly.

Steak with Tangy Herb Butter

The steaks you make from the bottom third of a chuck roast provide some of the best tasting beef you can find. Why not give them an all-out elegant treatment! When you serve them with the delicious parsley-watercress butter given here, an accompaniment of baked potatoes makes good use of any remaining butter.

Lower section blade-cut chuck roast, bone removed (see page 7)
½ tablespoon *each* butter or margarine and salad oil
Salt
Herb Butter (recipe follows)
Watercress

1. Trim and discard fat from meat; cut the piece of meat in half crosswise into two equal slices, each ¾ to 1 inch thick. If necessary, roll slightly and fasten with wooden picks to make more compact steaks.

2. Heat butter and oil together in a heavy frying pan until foamy; cook steaks quickly until well browned on each side (4 to 5 minutes per side). Remove to warm serving plates. Sprinkle with salt.

3. Serve topped with a chunk of Herb Butter, accompanied by a bouquet of watercress.

Makes 2 servings.

Herb Butter: Beat ¼ cup soft butter or margarine until fluffy; gradually beat in 1 tablespoon lemon juice until well combined, then mix in 2 tablespoons *each* finely chopped parsley and watercress, ½ teaspoon Worcestershire sauce and a dash of white pepper. Shape into a roll or a cube, wrap in plastic film and chill several hours to blend flavors.

Mustard and Pepper Steak

Here is that marvelously flavorsome and tender steak from the chuck again (see page 7), in a version for two that is so elegant it would do a French chef proud. Serve it with baked potatoes or noodles with butter and chopped parsley, and broiled tomato halves covered with melted cheese.

2 boneless steaks from blade-cut chuck roast (see page 7)
1 teaspoon whole white or black peppers, coarsely crushed
¼ teaspoon crumbled rosemary
1 tablespoon *each* butter or margarine and salad oil
Salt
1 tablespoon Dijon-style mustard
¼ cup *each* dry vermouth or white wine and whipping cream

1. Trim and discard fat from meat; if necessary, roll slightly and fasten with wooden picks to make more compact steaks. Mix crushed pepper and rosemary; press mixture into steaks on both sides.

2. Heat butter and oil together in a heavy frying pan until foamy; cook steaks quickly until well browned on each side, about 4 minutes per side. Remove to warm serving plates; sprinkle with salt. Pour off fat.

3. To pan in which steaks were cooked add mustard, vermouth and cream, stirring to blend well and loosen brown bits from pan. Boil, stirring until reduced and slightly thickened. Pour sauce over steaks.

Makes 2 servings.

Herb butter tops boneless steaks from chuck as well as baked potatoes in an elegant dish for two.

Gypsy-Style Steak

Mushrooms, onions and sweet red pepper strips in a sour cream sauce cover this rare steak. After the sour cream is added the sauce should be heated to *just below* the boiling point, since more heat may cause it to separate. Fluffy white rice is a natural accompaniment.

2 tablespoons butter or margarine
1 tablespoon salad oil
1 medium onion, finely chopped
1 sweet red pepper, seeded and cut in strips
¼ pound mushrooms, sliced
1 clove garlic, minced or pressed
4 boneless steaks from 2 blade-cut chuck roasts (see page 7)
Salt and paprika
⅓ cup dry white wine
½ cup sour cream
Chopped parsley, for garnish

1. In a large frying pan heat 1 tablespoon of the butter with salad oil. In it, cook onion, red pepper, mushrooms and garlic, stirring frequently, until tender; remove vegetable mixture from the pan.

2. Sprinkle steaks with salt and paprika. Add remaining butter to pan in which vegetables were cooked. Brown steaks quickly on both sides over high heat, about 4 minutes per side; remove to a warm serving platter.

3. Add wine to pan and cook quickly to reduce slightly, stirring in brown bits from pan. Reduce heat to moderate, mix in vegetables and cook until heated through. Over low heat, smoothly mix in sour cream (do not boil). Spoon sauce over steaks. Sprinkle with parsley.

Makes 4 servings.

Elegant Eye of Round Steaks

One way to make this compact cut of meat tender is to slice it thinly and pound it, and then brown the steaks very quickly so the meat will be rare and juicy. Accompany the steaks with slender French fries, tender-crisp green beans and a red wine, such as Zinfandel.

2 eyes of round from full-cut round steaks (see page 7), about 12 oz., with fat trimmed
Coarsely ground pepper and flour
1 tablespoon *each* butter or margarine and salad oil
Salt
¼ pound small mushrooms, quartered
2 shallots, finely chopped, *or* 2 tablespoons very finely chopped mild onion
¼ cup dry red wine
Chopped parsley

Accompany Gypsy-Style Steak with rice and lightly cooked zucchini to complement creamy red pepper sauce.

1. Freeze eye of round steaks partially, just until ice crystals begin to form. Slice each steak horizontally into 2 thin slices. Using the flat side of a meat mallet, pound steaks between pieces of waxed paper until they are about ¼ inch thick. Sprinkle with pepper and dust lightly with flour, shaking off excess.

2. Heat butter and oil in a large frying pan over high heat. Brown steaks very quickly on both sides; remove to a warm platter, sprinkle with salt and keep warm. Add mushrooms to pan and brown them quickly; stir in shallots and wine. Cook, stirring until most of the liquid is gone. Salt to taste, then spoon mushroom mixture over steaks. Sprinkle with parsley. Serve immediately with vegetables.

Makes 2 servings.

Steak and Onions for Two

Men love the sweetly pungent abundance of onions heaped over these quickly cooked steaks. German in origin, the steak and onions combine deliciously with butter-browned potatoes, cut into chunks, a green vegetable and a light red wine.

2 medium onions, thinly sliced
2 tablespoons butter or margarine
1 tablespoon salad oil
1 clove garlic, minced or pressed
2 boneless steaks from blade-cut chuck roast (see page 7)
Salt and white pepper
¼ cup dry white wine
Chopped parsley, for garnish

1. Separate onions into rings. In a 9 to 10-inch frying pan heat 1 tablespoon of the butter with oil. Add onions and garlic and cook slowly over low heat, stirring occasionally, until onions are limp and golden, 20 to 25 minutes. Increase heat to brown onions slightly; remove onions from pan and keep them warm in a 250° oven.

2. Sprinkle steaks with salt and pepper. Add remaining butter to same pan. Brown steaks quickly on both sides over moderately high heat, 3 to 4 minutes per side; remove to warm serving plates. Add wine to pan and cook quickly to reduce by about half, stirring in brown bits from pan. Reduce heat to moderate and mix in onions. Spoon onion mixture over steaks. Sprinkle with parsley.

Makes 2 servings.

Beef Stroganoff

After boning and trimming away fat, you should have about one-half pound meat from the top section (or flatiron muscle) of a typical 5-pound blade chuck roast. This recipe uses that section from two roasts.

- **1 pound beef chuck from atop blade bone, fat trimmed (see page 7)**
- **2 tablespoons butter or margarine**
- **1 tablespoon salad oil**
- **¼ pound mushrooms, sliced**
- **1 small onion, finely chopped**
- **¾ teaspoon salt**
- **1 teaspoon Worcestershire sauce**
  Dash *each* paprika and white pepper
- **½ cup sour cream**
  Chopped parsley, for garnish
  Noodles

1. Slice meat across the grain about ¼ inch thick; cut into bite-size strips.

2. Heat 1 tablespoon of the butter with oil in a large frying pan over moderately high heat until foamy. Add mushrooms and onion and cook quickly, stirring often, until browned. Remove mushroom mixture from pan with a slotted spoon and reserve.

3. To the pan add 1 tablespoon more butter, if needed. Add strips of meat and cook over high heat, turning meat and shaking pan, just until meat browns. Remove pan from heat; stir in mushroom mixture, salt, Worcestershire, paprika, pepper and sour cream.

4. Return pan to low heat, stirring constantly, just until sauce is heated through (do not allow to boil). Sprinkle with parsley; serve with noodles.

Makes 3 to 4 servings.

Shish Kebab Sauté

With a basis of boneless top round, this recipe takes the colorful elements of shish kebab and combines them as a quick-cooking sauté to serve with rice or a pilaf.

- **1½ to 2 pounds boneless top round**
  Red Wine Marinade (recipe follows)
- **1 medium onion, quartered and thinly sliced**
- **5 tablespoons butter or margarine**
- **1 green pepper, quartered, seeded and cut into crosswise strips**
- **½ pound mushrooms, quartered**
- **1 medium tomato, cut in 8 wedges**
  Salt

1. Trim fat and cut steak across the grain into bite-size strips about ¼ inch thick and ¾ to 1 inch wide. Place in marinade in a shallow bowl; cover and chill 2 to 3 hours or longer. Drain meat well on paper towels, reserving marinade for use later.

2. Cook onion in 2 tablespoons of the butter or margarine in a large frying pan over medium heat until it is lightly browned. Add green pepper; cook, stirring, until limp and bright green. Remove and reserve the vegetables. Brown mushrooms in 2 tablespoons more butter in the same pan; add to green pepper mixture. In remaining butter cook steak strips quickly, about a third at a time, turning with tongs just until browned on both sides.

3. Return all the steak and vegetables to the pan with tomato wedges and 2 tablespoons of the reserved marinade. Cook, stirring lightly, just until mixture is heated through. Salt to taste.

Makes 6 servings.

Red Wine Marinade: Thoroughly mix ½ cup dry red wine, 2 tablespoons salad oil, 1 tablespoon Worcestershire sauce, 1 clove garlic (minced or pressed), 1 teaspoon onion salt, ¼ teaspoon crumbled rosemary, ⅛ teaspoon thyme and a dash pepper. (*Note:* Marinade can be refrigerated and reused.)

Colorful vegetables are sautéed quickly with red wine-marinated boneless top round steak strips.

Joe's Special

This meal-in-one-skillet dish is a San Francisco favorite. The mushrooms are a nice addition, but you can omit them to keep the cost down. For a quick supper, it needs few accompaniments—simply a crusty loaf of French bread and a hearty red wine.

1 pound ground beef, crumbled
1½ tablespoons olive oil or salad oil
1 large onion, finely chopped
1 clove garlic, minced or pressed
¼ pound mushrooms, sliced (optional)
1 teaspoon salt
⅛ teaspoon *each* pepper and oregano
Dash nutmeg
2 cups chopped fresh spinach
3 eggs
Freshly grated Parmesan cheese

1. Brown ground beef well in heated oil in a large heavy frying pan over high heat. Add onion, garlic and mushrooms (if used); reduce heat and continue cooking, stirring occasionally, until onion is soft. Stir in seasonings and spinach; cook about 5 minutes longer, stirring several times.

2. Add eggs to meat mixture; stir quickly over low heat just until eggs begin to set. Serve immediately. Sprinkle cheese over each serving to taste.

Makes 3 to 4 servings.

Beef Fondue

Using boneless top round that has been tenderized, you can serve an elegant beef fondue to cook at the table very economically. Accompany it with warm French bread and a green salad.

1½ to 2 pounds boneless top round
Unseasoned powdered meat tenderizer
2 cups salad oil
Salt and pepper
Spicy Garlic Mayonnaise (recipe follows)

1. Trim fat from meat and cut it into about ¾-inch cubes. Sprinkle with meat tenderizer and let stand at room temperature about 30 minutes, according to tenderizer directions.

2. Heat oil on top of range or in an electric fondue pot to about 360°. If done on range top, transfer to fondue pot over alcohol or canned heat burner.

3. At the table, each person cooks steak cubes, one at a time, on fondue forks or bamboo skewers. Allow 20 to 30 seconds, depending on heat of oil, for meat to brown lightly on outside, remain juicy and rare in center. Transfer cooked meat to plate, sprinkle with salt and pepper, spear with another fork (metal fondue forks get

too hot from cooking to be used for eating), and dip into Garlic Mayonnaise or other favorite fondue sauces.

Makes 4 to 6 servings.

Spicy Garlic Mayonnaise: In blender container combine 1 egg, 2 teaspoons Dijon-style mustard, 1 teaspoon paprika, 1 clove garlic (minced or pressed), ½ teaspoon salt, 2 tablespoons white wine vinegar and ¼ cup olive oil. Cover and whirl at low speed. Immediately uncover and pour in ¾ cup salad oil in a slow, steady stream. Whirl until thick and smooth. To Garlic Mayonnaise in a mixing bowl add 1 tablespoon *each* chili sauce and drained capers, 1 teaspoon Worcestershire sauce, 2 tablespoons snipped fresh chives or thinly sliced green onions and 2 tablespoons chopped sour pickle. Cover and chill.

Makes about 1½ cups.

Homemade garlic mayonnaise makes a tangy dip for beef fondue.

Hamburgers au Poivre

Coated with coarsely crushed pepper and flamed with brandy for a dramatic finishing touch, these hamburgers are definitely elegant fare. Serve them with tiny green peas and thin, crisp French fried potatoes.

   1½ pounds ground lean beef
   ½ teaspoon garlic powder
   1 teaspoon *each* salt, Worcestershire sauce and Dijon-style mustard
   1 teaspoon whole black peppers, coarsely crushed
   1 tablespoon *each* butter or margarine and salad oil
   ⅓ cup regular-strength beef broth (homemade or canned)
   2 tablespoons very finely chopped onion
   3 tablespoons brandy
   Watercress, for garnish

1. Lightly mix ground beef, garlic powder, salt, Worcestershire sauce and mustard. Shape into 4 large patties. Rub and press crushed pepper into both sides of the patties. Cover with waxed paper and let stand at least 30 minutes.

2. In a large heavy frying pan heat combined butter and oil over moderately high heat until foamy. Cook meat patties in the heated mixture for 2½ to 4 minutes on each side until well browned. Remove to a warm platter and keep warm.

3. Pour off the cooking fat. Stir broth and onions into the pan, stirring in brown bits. Boil, stirring until most of the liquid is gone. Remove from heat, add brandy, and swirl to mix and heat it slightly. Ignite and spoon, flaming, over burgers. Garnish with bouquets of watercress. Serve immediately.

Makes 4 servings.

Mediterranean Parslied Meatballs

Meatballs are always a favorite family meal, but with a little imagination they can be elegant enough for company, too. These light textured meatballs have a definite Greek influence, with oregano, lots of chopped parsley and a tart lemon butter drizzled over them. Serve the meatballs with rice and sautéed zucchini.

   1 medium onion, chopped
   ¼ cup water
   1 egg
   ¼ cup milk
   ⅓ cup fine dry bread crumbs
   1 clove garlic, minced or pressed
   1 teaspoon salt
   ¼ teaspoon crumbled oregano
   ⅛ teaspoon pepper
   1 pound ground lean beef
   ½ cup chopped parsley
   2 tablespoons butter or margarine
   2 tablespoons lemon juice

1. Place onion in a small pan with water. Cook, covered, until onion is transparent; drain. In a mixing bowl, beat egg with milk. Mix in bread crumbs, garlic, salt, oregano and pepper; let stand for a few minutes. Then lightly mix in drained onion, ground beef and parsley. Shape into meatballs about 1½ inches in diameter.

2. Slowly brown meatballs on all sides in heated butter in a large frying pan. Remove to a warm serving dish. To pan drippings add lemon juice; stir to loosen brown bits. Pour pan drippings over meatballs. Sprinkle with a little additional chopped parsley.

Makes 3 to 4 servings.

Scandinavian Meatballs

These beef-and-pork meatballs are gently spiced and served in a creamy sauce that is good with either noodles or rice, dark rye bread and a salad with dilled cucumbers.

   1 egg
   1½ cups milk
   ½ cup fine dry bread crumbs
   1 teaspoon *each* salt and sugar
   ¼ teaspoon *each* ground ginger, nutmeg and allspice
   1 pound ground lean beef
   ½ pound ground pork
   1 small onion, finely chopped
   ¼ cup butter or margarine
   1 tablespoon flour
   Chopped parsley, for garnish

1. In a mixing bowl, beat egg with ½ cup of the milk. Blend in bread crumbs, salt, sugar and spices. Thoroughly mix in ground meats and onion. Shape into meatballs about the size of walnuts.

2. Brown meatballs well in heated butter in a large heavy frying pan. As they brown, remove them to a warm dish in a 250° oven to keep warm.

3. Pour off all but about 1 tablespoon of the fat. Cook flour in same pan, stirring, until bubbly and lightly browned. Gradually mix in the remaining 1 cup milk, cooking until thickened and smooth. Salt to taste. Return meatballs to pan, cover and simmer 15 minutes. Sprinkle with parsley.

Makes 4 to 6 servings.

Creamy Scandinavian meatballs are good with noodles or rice and a dilled cucumber salad.

Quick Liver and Mushrooms

One thing liver doesn't need is over-cooking. Quickly browned, the center stays pink and moist and the texture and flavor are at their best. Here it is further enhanced by a light sauce with onions, mushrooms and wine.

1 pound sliced young beef liver, cut in serving pieces
Salt, pepper and flour
3 tablespoons butter or margarine
1 small onion, finely chopped
1 can (4 oz.) mushroom pieces and stems, drained
2 tablespoons lemon juice
¼ cup dry white wine
Chopped parsley, for garnish

1. Sprinkle liver with salt and pepper; coat lightly with flour. Heat 2 tablespoons of the butter in a large frying pan. In it brown liver quickly on both sides; remove to a warm serving platter, and keep warm in a 250° oven.

2. Add remaining 1 tablespoon butter to pan and in it brown onion and mushrooms; stir in lemon juice and wine. Bring to boiling and cook, stirring to mix in brown bits in pan, until slightly reduced. Spoon mushroom sauce over liver; sprinkle with parsley.

Makes 3 to 4 servings.

Alpine Liver Strips in Wine Cream Sauce

This Swiss favorite features quickly cooked bite-sized strips of calf or young beef liver in a winey cream sauce. Accompany it with fresh noodles or hash brown potatoes and steamed broccoli with browned butter.

1½ pounds sliced young beef or calf liver, cut into 2 by ½-inch strips
Salt, white pepper and nutmeg
Flour
¼ cup butter or margarine
2 tablespoons vegetable oil
2 shallots, chopped, or 2 tablespoons very finely chopped onion
½ cup dry white wine
¾ cup whipping cream
Chopped parsley, for garnish

1. Sprinkle liver with salt, pepper and nutmeg; coat lightly with flour, shaking off excess. In a large heavy frying pan heat 2 tablespoons of the butter with the oil over moderately high heat until foamy. In it brown half the liver, cooking just until well browned on both sides. Remove liver and keep it warm. Add 1 tablespoon more butter to pan; heat, and then cook remaining liver. Add it to previously cooked liver.

2. Add remaining 1 tablespoon butter to pan. In it cook shallots until lightly browned. Add wine and cream; cook, stirring briskly, until sauce boils and is reduced by about half. Salt to taste.

3. Return liver and its juices to sauce, stirring over medium heat until heated through. Sprinkle with chopped parsley to serve.

Makes 4 to 6 servings.

Italian Veal Sauté

Although most cuts of veal are usually fairly expensive, occasionally you can find a good value in a boneless roast. Cut it up yourself—in slices for scaloppine, or in strips or cubes for a quick sauté such as this—and you are bound to save.

2 pounds boneless veal, cut in small cubes
Salt, white pepper, nutmeg and flour
3 tablespoons butter or margarine
2 tablespoons olive oil or salad oil
1 medium onion, finely chopped
½ teaspoon Italian herb seasoning blend
2 cloves garlic, minced or pressed
½ cup dry white wine or regular-strength chicken broth (homemade or canned)
¼ cup chopped parsley
¼ cup dry Marsala or sherry
Lemon wedges

1. Sprinkle veal with salt, pepper and nutmeg; coat cubes lightly with flour, shaking off excess. Heat 2 tablespoons of the butter with oil in a large frying pan. Brown veal, about half at a time, on all sides, removing cubes as they brown.

2. When all the veal is well browned, add remaining 1 tablespoon butter and brown onion lightly. Return veal to pan. Sprinkle with herb mixture and garlic, and pour on wine or broth. Cover and simmer 15 minutes. Uncover; stir in parsley and Marsala or sherry. Salt to taste. Accompany with lemon wedges.

Makes 6 servings.

Veal Kidneys in Sherry and Mustard Sauce

Kidneys are another variety meat that benefits from fast cooking. Overcooked, they can become strong-tasting and tough, but when quickly sautéed they are just the opposite. Try them served over rice or buttered English muffins in a robustly flavored sauce that is a good match for their distinctive taste.

6 veal kidneys (about 1 lb.)
Salt and white pepper
3 tablespoons butter or margarine
¼ pound mushrooms, sliced
¼ cup finely chopped onion
¼ cup dry sherry
2 teaspoons Dijon-style mustard
½ cup sour cream
Chopped parsley

1. To prepare kidneys, cut away fatty membrane, then cut in slices ½ inch thick. Sprinkle with salt and pepper.

2. Heat 2 tablespoons of the butter over moderately high heat. In it cook mushrooms until browned; remove and reserve them. Add a little more butter, and in it cook onion lightly. Add kidneys and remaining butter and cook quickly, stirring, just until firm and lightly browned. Add kidneys to mushrooms.

3. To pan, add sherry and mustard, cooking and stirring until smooth and slightly reduced. Return kidney mixture to cooking pan. Over low heat, stir sour cream into kidneys, cooking just until heated through (*do not boil*). Salt to taste. Sprinkle with parsley.

Makes 4 servings.

Creamy Pork and Apple Sauté

Lean pork can substitute for veal in many dishes. Cooked with apple wedges, wine and cream and served with hot rice or noodles, it is delicate and tender.

1½ to 2 pounds lean, boneless pork butt
⅓ cup flour
1½ teaspoons salt
½ teaspoon *each* paprika and nutmeg
⅛ teaspoon white pepper
2 to 3 tablespoons butter or margarine
1 tablespoon salad oil
1 small onion, finely chopped
2 medium-sized tart cooking apples, peeled and cut in ½-inch wedges
¾ cup dry white wine
½ cup whipping cream
Chopped parsley, for garnish

1. Cut pork into thin strips about 2 inches long and ½ to ¾ inch wide. Mix flour, salt, paprika, nutmeg and pepper. Lightly coat pork strips with the flour mixture, shaking off excess. Heat 2 tablespoons of the butter with the oil in a large frying pan over moderately high heat. In it brown pork strips on all sides, about a third at a time. Remove them when they are well browned.

2. Add more butter, if needed. Cook onion, stirring occasionally, until lightly browned. Return pork and any juices to the frying pan. Add apple wedges. Pour on wine and cream. Bring to boiling, reduce heat, cover and simmer for about 20 minutes, until pork is tender. With a slotted spoon, remove pork and apples to a warm serving dish.

3. Bring pan juices to boiling and stir briskly over high heat until sauce is smooth; salt to taste. Pour over pork and apples. Sprinkle with parsley.

Makes 4 servings.

Pita Bread Sandwich Party

Stuffed with a saucy ground lamb mixture and topped with cool yogurt and crisp, fresh vegetables, the hot sandwiches featured in this informal party menu might be described as Middle Eastern tacos.

They are good family fare, too. The basic recipe makes four servings. For a party, double it, using a large can (15 oz.) tomato sauce. The recipe can also be multiplied by three, using one 8-ounce and one 15-ounce can tomato sauce.

**Ground Lamb in Pita Bread
Golden Rice Salad
Orange-Lemon Pound Cake
Nuts and Fruits:
Almonds and Walnuts in Shells,
Tangelos, Bananas, Dates, Dried
Papaya Strips, Apples, Grapes
Chilled Dry Rosé Wine or Beer**

Golden Rice Salad

2½ cups water
  1 teaspoon *each* olive oil or salad oil, turmeric and salt
1¼ cups long grain rice
  1 cup thawed frozen peas
  1 jar (4 oz.) sliced pimiento, drained
  ¼ cup *each* finely chopped parsley and sliced green onions (use part of tops)
  2 teaspoons drained capers
  Lemon Mayonnaise (recipe follows)
  Romaine or leaf lettuce

1. In a 2-quart saucepan combine water, oil, turmeric and salt; bring to boiling. Gradually pour in rice. Cover, reduce heat and simmer for 22 to 25 minutes, until rice is just tender. Chill thoroughly.

2. Fluff chilled rice with a fork. Lightly mix in peas, pimiento, parsley,

Serve colorful rice salad with sandwiches.

Pita bread halves hold spicy lamb filling.

green onions, capers and mayonnaise. Cover and chill for several hours to blend flavors.

3. Serve in a bowl lined with romaine or leaf lettuce, sprinkled with additional sliced green onions.

Makes 6 to 8 servings.

Lemon Mayonnaise: In blender combine 1 egg yolk, 1 teaspoon *each* grated lemon peel and Dijon-style mustard, ½ teaspoon garlic salt, 2 teaspoons lemon juice, 1 tablespoon white vinegar, dash cayenne and 3 tablespoons olive oil. Cover and turn motor on low speed. Immediately uncover and pour in ⅔ cup salad oil in a slow, steady stream. Whirl until thick and smooth. Makes just under 1 cup of mayonnaise.

Ground Lamb in Pita Bread

  **1 pound ground lamb, crumbled
  1 medium onion, chopped
  1 clove garlic, minced or pressed
  1 can (8 oz.) tomato sauce
  ¾ teaspoon salt
  ½ teaspoon ground cumin
  ¼ teaspoon *each* crumbled oregano and ground allspice
  4 pita breads
  Unflavored yogurt, chopped cucumber, slivered green pepper and thinly sliced green onions (use part of tops)**

1. Brown lamb in its own drippings in a large heavy frying pan. Spoon off excess fat. Mix in onion and cook, stirring, until lightly browned. Stir in garlic, tomato sauce, salt, cumin, oregano and allspice. Bring to boiling, cover frying pan, reduce heat and simmer gently 15 minutes.

2. Meanwhile, wrap pita breads in foil and heat in a 350° oven 10 to 15 minutes. Cut in halves. Spoon in ground lamb mixture. At the table, add yogurt, cucumber, green pepper and green onions to taste.

Makes 4 servings.

Orange-Lemon Pound Cake

2¼ cups sifted all-purpose flour
  ¼ teaspoon baking soda
2¼ cups sugar
1½ cups (¾ lb.) soft butter or margarine
  2 tablespoons lemon juice
  1 tablespoon *each* vanilla and orange flower water
  1 teaspoon *each* grated orange and lemon peel
  7 eggs, separated (at room temperature)
  ½ teaspoon cream of tartar
  Powdered sugar

1. Mix flour with soda and 1¼ cups of the sugar. In a large bowl with mixer at low speed, add flour mixture to butter, mixing just until combined. Blend in lemon juice, vanilla, orange flower water and orange and lemon peels. Add egg yolks, one at a time, blending after each addition.

2. Beat egg whites with cream of tartar until frothy. Gradually add remaining 1 cup sugar, beating constantly, until soft peaks form. Gently but thoroughly fold egg whites into batter. Spread in a floured and greased 10-cup fluted tube pan, about 10 inches in diameter.

3. Bake in a 325° oven for about 1 hour and 10 minutes, until cake begins to pull away from sides of pan and tests done when a long bamboo skewer is inserted in thickest part. Turn off heat and leave cake in the oven for 15 minutes longer.

4. Remove pan to a cooling rack and let cake stand at room temperature for about 15 minutes. Then carefully invert cake onto rack to complete cooling. While still warm, sprinkle with powdered sugar. When cool, wrap in foil and let stand for up to 24 hours before serving.

5. Sprinkle with additional powdered sugar before serving.

Makes 10 to 12 servings.

The informal sandwich party shown on the facing page is capped by a dessert of sugar-dusted, citrus-flavored pound cake.

One of the most elegant ways to serve boneless chicken breasts is in a wine-cream sauce with seedless grapes. Accompany the dish with rice, a simple green vegetable and a fruity white wine.

Chicken Breasts with Grapes

Once you have mastered the technique of boning chicken breasts, you can save money at the meat counter again and again. Boneless chicken breasts can be quickly and elegantly cooked in an almost limitless variety of popular ways. Follow the step-by-step directions on page 9, and after a few tries you will be able to prepare classic dishes like this one in no time at all. Accompany the chicken breasts with fluffy rice and a fruity white wine such as Chenin Blanc.

 3 **whole chicken breasts (6 halves, about 3 lbs. in all), halved, boned and skinned**
   Salt and nutmeg
 2 **tablespoons butter or margarine**
 1 **tablespoon orange marmalade**
 ¼ **teaspoon crumbled tarragon**
 1 **green onion, thinly sliced (use part of top)**
 ⅓ **cup dry white wine**
 1 **cup seedless grapes**
 ¼ **cup whipping cream**

1. Sprinkle chicken breasts with salt and nutmeg. Brown lightly in heated butter in a large frying pan. Add marmalade, tarragon, green onion and wine. Cover, reduce heat and simmer 10 minutes; add grapes, cover again and continue cooking about 10 minutes longer, until chicken is cooked through (test with a small sharp knife in thickest part).

2. Using a slotted spoon, remove chicken and grapes to a warm serving dish; keep warm. Add cream to liquid in pan. Bring to boiling, stirring, and cook until reduced and slightly thickened. Salt to taste. Pour sauce over chicken.

Makes 4 to 6 servings.

Chicken Breasts with Mushrooms, Swiss Cheese and White Wine

The speed with which chicken breasts can be cooked makes them an ideal choice for a main dish that cooks in the time it takes for a before-dinner drink. Cooked with its own luscious sauce, this entrée is delicious accompanied by green beans and butter-browned new potatoes.

 3 **whole chicken breasts (6 halves, about 3 lbs. in all), halved, boned and skinned (see page 9)**
   Salt, white pepper and nutmeg
 2 **tablespoons butter or margarine**
 1 **tablespoon salad oil**
 ¼ **pound mushrooms, sliced**
 2 **shallots, chopped, *or* 2 tablespoons very finely chopped mild onion**
 ½ **cup dry white wine**
 ½ **cup shredded aged natural Swiss cheese**
 ½ **cup whipping cream**
   Dash of paprika
   Cherry tomatoes and thinly sliced green onions, for garnish

1. Sprinkle chicken breasts on all sides with salt, white pepper and nutmeg. In a large frying pan heat together butter and oil. Add chicken breasts and brown lightly; turn, add mushrooms and shallots around chicken, and continue cooking until chicken breasts are lightly browned on both sides.

2. Pour on wine; cover and simmer 15 to 20 minutes, just until chicken is cooked through. Using a slotted spoon, remove chicken to a warm serving dish; keep warm. Bring liquid to boiling, stirring until reduced by about half. Mix in cheese, cream and paprika. Cook over moderate heat, stirring, until cheese melts and sauce is slightly thickened. Salt sauce to taste. Spoon over chicken. Garnish with cherry tomatoes and a sprinkling of green onions.

Makes 4 to 6 servings.

Hungarian Chicken Breasts

Red and green pepper strips give paprika seasoned chicken breasts a colorful embellishment. Serve with twisted noodles or rice.

3 whole chicken breasts (6 halves, about 3 lbs. in all), halved, boned and skinned (see page 9)
Salt, white pepper and flour
1 teaspoon *each* butter or margarine and salad oil
1 small onion, finely chopped
1 *each* red and green bell pepper, quartered, seeded and cut into thin crosswise strips
1 small can (2 oz.) mushroom pieces and stems, drained
1 teaspoon paprika
⅓ cup dry white wine
⅔ cup sour cream

1. Sprinkle chicken breasts lightly with salt and pepper. Coat with flour, shaking off excess. In a large frying pan brown chicken breasts well on both sides in a mixture of heated butter and oil. Top with onion, red and green pepper strips and mushrooms; sprinkle with paprika. Pour on wine. Bring to boiling, reduce heat, cover and simmer about 20 minutes, until chicken is cooked through (test with a small sharp knife in thickest part). Using a slotted spoon, remove chicken and vegetables to a heated serving dish; keep warm.

2. Bring cooking liquid to boiling, loosening brown bits from pan; cook until reduced by about half. Remove from heat; stir in sour cream. Return to low heat just to heat through (*do not boil*). Salt to taste. Pour sauce over chicken breasts and vegetables.

Makes 4 to 6 servings.

Sweet-and-Sour Chicken Wings

When you cut up whole frying chickens, save the wings for your soup kettle—or this tart and colorful main dish, served with steamed rice or Chinese noodles.

2 pounds chicken wings
2 tablespoons salad oil
1 onion, thinly sliced and separated into rings
1 carrot, thinly sliced
1 clove garlic, minced or pressed
⅓ cup vinegar
⅓ cup firmly packed brown sugar
¼ cup *each* catsup and unsweetened pineapple juice
1 tablespoon soy sauce
1 green pepper, halved, seeded and cut into 1-inch squares
2 teaspoons cornstarch, smoothly mixed with 1 tablespoon water

1. Separate each chicken wing (at joints) into 3 pieces; discard (or reserve for soup) wing tips. Brown well, about a third at a time, in heated oil in a large frying pan; pour off fat. Return all browned chicken wings to pan.

2. Add onion, carrot and garlic. Mix together until smooth the vinegar, brown sugar, catsup, pineapple juice and soy sauce; pour over chicken and vegetables. Cover and cook for 15 minutes; add green pepper and cook for about 5 minutes longer, until chicken is cooked through and carrots are tender-crisp. Remove chicken and vegetables to a warm serving dish.

3. Remove sauce from heat; smoothly blend in cornstarch mixture. Return to heat and cook, stirring, until thickened and clear. Salt to taste. Pour sauce over chicken and serve.

Makes 3 to 4 servings.

Spaghetti with Chicken Livers

Here is an impromptu spaghetti sauce that is nice for a late evening supper with bread sticks, a butter or leaf lettuce salad with an herb dressing and a robust red wine.

2 slices bacon, diced
1 pound chicken livers, cut in halves
1 onion, finely chopped
1 large can (4 oz.) mushroom pieces and stems, drained
1 clove garlic, minced or pressed
1 can (6 oz.) tomato paste
1 can (13¾ oz.) regular-strength chicken broth, *or* 1¾ cups homemade chicken broth
1 teaspoon Italian herb seasoning blend
½ teaspoon *each* salt and sugar
Dash pepper
¼ cup chopped parsley
1 pound spaghetti, cooked and drained
2 tablespoons soft butter or margarine
Freshly grated Parmesan cheese

1. Cook bacon in a large frying pan until crisp and browned; remove with a slotted spoon and drain on paper towels. In bacon drippings, cook chicken livers, about half at a time, until nicely browned on all sides; remove from pan and reserve.

2. To pan add onion and mushrooms; cook until tender and beginning to brown. Mix in garlic, tomato paste, chicken broth, herb seasoning, salt, sugar and pepper. Bring to boiling, reduce heat and simmer, uncovered, for 15 to 20 minutes, stirring occasionally.

3. Return chicken livers and bacon to sauce; cook 5 minutes longer. Stir in parsley. Lightly mix hot cooked spaghetti with butter; top with chicken liver sauce. Add grated Parmesan cheese to taste.

Makes 4 to 6 servings.

Golden Turkey Breast Parmigiana

Turkey parts are often reasonably priced. Bone, skin and slice turkey breast to use as you would veal scaloppine (save the bones for the soup on page 54). It is delicious marinated, then lightly coated with flour and Parmesan cheese and sautéed.

2 pounds turkey breast
3 tablespoons lemon juice
⅓ cup olive oil or salad oil
¼ teaspoon *each* salt and white pepper
½ cup *each* flour and grated Parmesan cheese
6 tablespoons butter or margarine (approximately)
Lemon wedges

1. Bone and skin turkey breast. Place, smooth-side up, on a cutting board. Cut meat across the grain into large slices about ½ inch thick. Place turkey pieces, one at a time, between two sheets of waxed paper; pound each with flat side of a meat mallet to flatten to about ¼-inch thickness.

2. Beat or shake together lemon juice, oil, salt and pepper until well combined. Pour over pounded turkey in a shallow dish; cover and refrigerate for about 1 hour. Drain turkey.

3. Coat turkey pieces generously with mixture of flour and cheese. Heat 4 tablespoons of the butter in a large frying pan. Quickly sauté turkey slices, 4 or 5 at a time, until lightly browned on each side, 3 to 5 minutes for each side, adding more butter as needed. Keep cooked turkey warm in a 250° oven while cooking remainder. When cooked, serve at once with lemon.

Makes 4 to 6 servings.

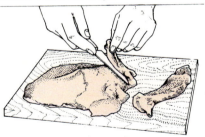

Boning a half turkey breast is much like boning chicken. Cut away rib bones, if any, then cut out wishbone.

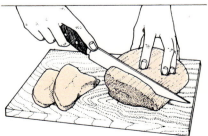

Slice across grain, about ½ inch thick.

Stir-Frying

Many familiar Chinese dishes are prepared by stir-frying, a quick-cooking technique similar to sautéeing. For stir-frying, ingredients are cut in bite-sized pieces that will cook quickly and in about the same amount of time. High heat is used for stir-frying, and—as the name suggests—foods must be stirred or lifted frequently as they cook. Even if you are not skilled at Chinese cooking, you can easily borrow the stir-fry idea for quick-cooking main dishes. It's not necessary to have any special equipment. Although a wok is the pan designed for this style of cooking, many simple dishes such as the four that follow can be cooked in a standard frying pan or in an electric skillet. The important thing is to have all the ingredients ready.

Szechwan Chicken and Peanuts

People who enjoy bold seasonings are discovering that Szechwan-style Chinese food can be quite as satisfyingly mouth-searing as the most flamboyant Mexican cooking. While this chicken dish won't make you breathe fire, it does have the perceptible heat that only dried chile peppers can generate. Accompany it with steamed rice.

2 whole chicken breasts (4 halves, about 2 lbs. in all), halved, boned and skinned (see page 9)
2 teaspoons cornstarch
¼ teaspoon ground ginger
2 tablespoons *each* water and dry sherry
¼ cup soy sauce
1 tablespoon *each* sugar and white vinegar
2 cloves garlic, minced or pressed
5 small dried hot red chile peppers
3 tablespoons salad oil
½ cup dry roast peanuts
1 large green pepper, quartered, seeded and cut in ¾-inch squares

1. Cut chicken into bite-sized ½-inch-wide strips. Mix cornstarch, ginger, water, sherry, soy sauce, sugar, vinegar and garlic until smooth. Slit red peppers; remove and discard seeds.

2. In a large heavy frying pan or wok, heat oil. Add chile peppers and peanuts. Cook, stirring until peanuts are browned; remove peanuts and peppers with a slotted spoon, discarding peppers. Drain peanuts on paper towels.

3. Add chicken strips to pan and cook, stirring, until chicken is white and opaque-looking throughout. Add green peppers and cook, stirring, about 2

If you enjoy the fiery flavors of Szechwan Chinese food, try this stir-fried chicken with peanuts.

minutes longer. Stir soy sauce mixture and add it to chicken. Cook, stirring, until thickened and clear. Return peanuts to pan and continue cooking until peppers are tender-crisp.

Makes 3 to 4 servings.

Gingered Flank Steak with Snow Peas

Flank steak is frequently mentioned as a less costly cut of beef. While it is not as expensive as some loin cuts, it is by no means a rock-bottom bargain either. The cost-per-pound of flank steak is likely to be double that of any other meat suggested in this book! However, it is lean and boneless, and delicious in a stir-fry dish such as this. (If you prefer to use a less expensive cut than flank steak, substitute an equal weight of boneless chuck, using the flatiron muscle atop the blade bone: see page 7). Serve with rice.

1 pound flank steak, partially frozen
⅓ cup water
2½ teaspoons cornstarch
2 tablespoons dry sherry
¼ cup soy sauce
2 teaspoons grated peeled fresh ginger, *or* ½ teaspoon ground ginger
1 clove garlic, minced or pressed
3 tablespoons salad oil
½ pound mushrooms, sliced
½ pound edible-pod peas, stems and strings removed

1. Slice flank steak diagonally into thin strips about 1 inch wide and 2 inches long. Mix water, cornstarch, sherry, soy sauce, ginger and garlic until cornstarch dissolves.

2. In a large frying pan or wok, heat 2 tablespoons of the oil; in it brown beef strips quickly on both sides, about half at a time, removing them as soon as they brown.

3. When all the beef is browned and removed from pan, add remaining 1 tablespoon oil. In it brown mushrooms lightly, stirring; mix in peas, stirring until bright green. Add seasoned cornstarch liquid and cook, stirring, until thickened and clear. Return beef strips to pan and cook just until heated through. Serve immediately.

Makes 4 servings.

Pork with Tofu

Tofu, or soy bean curd, is creamy looking and mild flavored. High in protein, yet relatively inexpensive in stores featuring Oriental ingredients, it can be used to stretch higher-priced meats. Like pasta, *tofu* has a way of setting off the fuller-flavored foods usually cooked with it. Serve the mixture in shallow soup bowls atop rice.

1 pound lean boneless pork butt
1 tablespoon salad oil
½ cup soy sauce
2 tablespoons sugar
¼ cup water
1 medium onion, thinly sliced and separated into rings
1 clove garlic, minced or pressed
2 teaspoons grated peeled fresh ginger, *or* ½ teaspoon ground ginger
2 slices *tofu* or soy bean cake (about 12 oz.), cut in 1-inch cubes
1 bunch (6 to 8) green onions, cut in 1-inch pieces (use part of tops)

1. Thinly slice pork, then cut it in 1 by 2-inch strips; brown in heated oil in a large frying pan or wok.

2. Mix in soy sauce, sugar, water, onion, garlic and ginger. Bring to boiling, reduce heat and simmer, uncovered, 5 minutes.

3. Mix in tofu and cook just until heated through. Stir in green onions; serve immediately.

Makes 4 to 6 servings.

Lamb with Five-Spice and Green Onions

The dominant flavor in Chinese five-spice powder is anise (the mixture also includes fennel, cloves, cinnamon and pepper). It is especially complementary to this lean, tender lamb. Use lamb shoulder you have boned yourself (see page 20), freeze the rest for stew or curry.

1 pound lean boneless lamb shoulder, thinly sliced and cut in bite-size strips
¾ teaspoon Chinese five-spice powder
1 clove garlic, minced or pressed
2 tablespoons soy sauce
⅓ cup dry sherry
2 tablespoons salad oil
1 teaspoon cornstarch, smoothly mixed with 1 tablespoon water
1 bunch (6 to 8) green onions, cut in diagonal slices about ½-inch thick

1. Mix lamb with five-spice powder, garlic, soy sauce and sherry; cover and refrigerate 1 to 4 hours. Drain meat, reserving marinade.

2. Heat oil in a large heavy frying pan or wok, in it cook lamb, about half at a time, turning and stirring until it is just browned. Remove pan from heat; return all the cooked lamb to the pan. Blend cornstarch mixture into reserved marinade; add to meat.

3. Return to heat and cook, stirring, until sauce is thickened. Stir in green onions. Serve immediately.

Makes 3 to 4 servings.

Elegant Whole-Meal Soups

Full meals from the soup kettle offer many advantages: economy, make-ahead convenience and wonderful flavor. They make great parties, too!

When people reminisce about childhood and family cooking, some of the most mouthwatering nostalgia is evoked by memories of the homemade soups of mother's or grandmother's kitchen. And usually such recollections are touched with the satisfaction that comes of creating something marvelous from next to nothing—"In those days, butchers *gave* soup bones away."

These days, unfortunately, hardly anyone gives anything away, but the bony cuts of meat that make the best flavored and sturdiest soups are still relatively economical. And, as you have seen, some of the prudent cook's best buys at the meat counter include bones that can be put away in the freezer until the right time to make an honest, old-fashioned soup.

Main-dish soups make fine family meals and are less work than you might expect. Although they generally require several hours of cooking, a simmering soup needs virtually no attention. With meat or poultry, vegetables and potatoes, rice or noodles all in one bowl, it takes but a few accompaniments to turn your good soup into a full meal. Just add bread or crackers, a salad or crisp raw vegetable relishes and a simple dessert, if you wish. Suggestions for complete soup menus that are elegant enough for festive occasions begin on page 55.

Milanese Vegetable-Beef Soup

A sort of *minestrone* (translation: big soup), this soup boasts a grand assortment of vegetables; the most fragile are added just at the end, to retain their fresh texture and brilliant green color. At the table, sprinkle the hot soup with Parmesan cheese and pour in some red wine from a carafe.

Hungarian Goulash Soup (recipe, page 57), stars in a festive supper prepared by the author. The soup is accompanied by sour cream, rye bread and a butter lettuce salad.

3½ to 4-pound blade-cut chuck roast
2 tablespoons olive oil or salad oil
2 large sweet red onions, sliced and separated into rings
2 carrots, thinly sliced
2 stalks celery, thinly sliced
2 cloves garlic, minced or pressed
½ cup chopped parsley
1 tablespoon salt
1 teaspoon crumbled basil
2½ quarts water (10 cups)
1 can (1 lb.) tomatoes
1 medium boiling potato, thinly sliced
1 package (9 oz.) frozen Italian green beans, thawed
2 medium zucchini, thinly sliced
2 cups chopped fresh spinach
Shredded Parmesan cheese
Dry red wine in carafe

1. Cut chuck roast into large chunks, trimming and discarding as much fat as possible. Brown meat and bones well in heated oil in a large kettle (at least 6-quart size). Mix in onions, and cook until limp. Add carrots, celery, garlic, parsley, salt, basil and water. Bring to boiling, cover, reduce heat and simmer for about 3 hours, until meat is very tender and broth is flavorful.

2. Remove meat and bones with a slotted spoon. Discard bones and fat; return meat in chunks to soup. (At this point, soup may be covered and chilled until ready to serve; skim fat from surface.)

3. To soup add tomatoes (coarsely chopped) and their liquid and potato. Bring to a gentle boil and cook, uncovered, for about 30 minutes, until potato is tender. Add beans and zucchini and cook for about 10 minutes longer, just until tender. Stir in spinach and cook about 3 minutes. Salt to taste. Serve soup with Parmesan cheese to sprinkle over and wine to pour in to each diner's taste.

Makes 6 servings.

At the table, flavor vegetable soup with red wine, Parmesan cheese.

Beefy French Onion Soup

The traditional onion soup of the legendary Paris market, Les Halles, is a rich beef broth, dense with onions, crowned with cheese-laden toast and so filling it is *almost* a main dish. Here, to take it one rich step further, the broth is made with meaty beef shanks. All this soup needs to become a meal is a leafy salad with an oil and vinegar dressing and a robust red wine.

The broth can be prepared a day or more in advance.

3½ to 4 pounds beef shanks
  6 tablespoons butter or margarine
  1 tablespoon salad oil
  1 large onion, finely chopped
  2 large carrots, thinly sliced
  1 tablespoon salt
  ½ teaspoon whole black peppers
  5 sprigs parsley
  1 bay leaf
  2 quarts water
  8 medium onions, thinly sliced and separated into rings
  1 clove garlic, minced or pressed
  2 tablespoons flour
  1 cup dry white wine
  6 thick slices French bread
  1 cup *each* shredded Swiss and Parmesan cheese

1. In a large soup kettle (at least 6-quart size), brown beef shanks well on all sides in heated mixture of 1 tablespoon of the butter and oil. Add chopped onion, carrots, salt, black peppers, parsley, bay leaf and water. Bring to boiling, reduce heat, cover and simmer for about 3 hours, until broth is richly flavored.

2. Strain broth into a large bowl. When meat is cool enough to handle, return it and marrow from bones to broth in chunks; discard vegetables and bones. Chill soup; skim off fat (this much can be done 1 to 2 days ahead.)

3. In the same large soup kettle, heat remaining 5 tablespoons butter. Add sliced onions, cover and cook until limp, about 10 minutes. Uncover and cook over low heat, stirring frequently, until onions brown lightly, about 30 minutes longer. (Reduce heat if onions become too brown.) Stir in garlic and flour. Cook and stir until bubbly. Remove from heat and stir in about 1 quart of the broth. Return to heat, and mix in remaining broth with beef and wine. Bring to a gentle boil, cover, reduce heat and simmer until ready to serve. Salt to taste.

4. Meanwhile, place bread in a single layer on a baking sheet in a 250° oven. Toast for about 30 minutes, until bread is very dry and barely browned. Sprinkle about ⅓ cup of the mixed cheeses over each toast slice.

Crusty bread and cheese top onion soup.

5. To serve, ladle soup into heatproof bowls. Top each with a cheese-and-toast slice. Place under broiler, about 5 inches from heat, until cheese is melted and lightly browned, 3 to 5 minutes. Serve immediately.

Makes 6 servings.

Beef and Sauerkraut Soup

Crowded with vegetables and meat, this sauerkraut soup has a pleasantly tart flavor, enhanced by sour cream added at the table.

4 beef shanks (about 3 lbs.), fat trimmed
1 tablespoon *each* butter or margarine and salad oil
2 medium onions, finely chopped
1 carrot, shredded
1 large clove garlic, minced or pressed
1 can (1 lb.) sauerkraut
1 quart water
1 can (l lb.) tomatoes, coarsely chopped, liquid reserved
⅛ teaspoon pepper
1 bay leaf
  Salt
  Sour cream

1. Brown beef shanks on all sides in mixture of heated butter and oil in a 5½ to 6-quart Dutch oven. Mix in onions and carrot, stirring until limp. Add garlic, sauerkraut, water, tomatoes and their liquid, pepper and bay leaf. Bring to boiling, reduce heat, cover and simmer for about 3 hours or until meat is very tender.

2. Remove beef shanks with a slotted spoon. Discard bones and any fat. Return meat to soup in chunks. (At this point, soup may be covered and chilled until ready to serve; skim fat, if necessary.)

3. Reheat soup to serving temperature. Taste and add salt, if needed.

Makes 4 to 6 servings.

Corned Beef and Cabbage Soup

The richly flavored liquid in which corned beef has been cooked is the basis for an appealing soup that is simplicity itself. Shredded cabbage, added a few minutes before serving, stays colorfully green, fresh tasting and slightly crisp.

3½ to 4-pound corned beef brisket
  Water
1 bay leaf
1 cinnamon stick, broken into 2 or 3 pieces
1 tablespoon mixed pickling spices, tied in a square of cheesecloth
2 medium onions, thinly sliced and separated into rings
1 stalk celery, thinly sliced
1 small head (about 1½ lbs.) cabbage
  Sour cream
  Snipped fresh dill or dried dill weed

1. Rinse corned beef well under cold running water, then place in a 5 to 6-quart kettle or Dutch oven. Cover with 2 quarts water and bring to boiling; drain. Add bay leaf, cinnamon stick, pickling spices, onions and celery. Cover with 2 quarts hot water. Bring to boiling, cover, reduce heat and simmer for about 4 hours or until meat is very tender.

2. Remove corned beef; discard pickling spices and bay leaf. Cut corned beef into thick slices and return it to soup. Quarter cabbage and cut it in thin shreds. Add shredded cabbage to soup. Bring to boiling and cook, uncovered, for 2 to 3 minutes, just until cabbage is limp but still bright green. Serve immediately in broad soup bowls; top each serving with a dollop of sour cream and a sprinkling of fresh or dried dill, if you wish.

Makes 6 to 8 servings.

Top Corned Beef and Cabbage Soup with a dollop of sour cream.

Fresh Corn and Polish Sausage Chowder

Creamy and colorful, this quick soup features the crisp freshness of corn, green pepper and cabbage.

1½ pounds Polish sausage (_kielbasa_), sliced about ¼-inch thick
2 medium boiling potatoes, cut in ½-inch cubes
1 bay leaf
1 green pepper, seeded and chopped
1 small jar (2 oz.) sliced pimientos
1 medium onion, thinly sliced and separated into rings
1 can (13¾ oz.) regular-strength chicken broth, _or_ 1¾ cups homemade chicken broth
2 ears corn, cut from cobs (1½ to 2 cups)
2 cups shredded cabbage
2 cups milk
Salt, white pepper and paprika

1. Place sausage slices in a 4 to 6-quart kettle or Dutch oven; cook over medium heat, stirring, to brown sausage lightly in its own drippings. Spoon off fat. Add potatoes, bay leaf, green pepper, pimientos, onion and broth. Bring to boiling, reduce heat, cover and simmer for 20 to 25 minutes, until potatoes are tender.

2. Stir in corn and cabbage and boil gently, uncovered, about 3 minutes. Add milk. Heat slowly just until soup is steaming hot (do not boil). Season to taste with salt and white pepper. Sprinkle with paprika.

Makes 4 to 6 servings.

Quick Italian Sausage and Bean Soup

Aromatic with anise and other herbs, Italian sausage gives body to this easy, chili-like soup.

1 pound mild Italian-style pork sausages
1 large onion, finely chopped
1 clove garlic, minced or pressed
1 green pepper, seeded and chopped
1 teaspoon mixed Italian herb seasoning
1 can (1 lb.) tomatoes
1 can (8 oz.) tomato sauce
1 can (13¾ oz.) regular-strength beef broth, _or_ 1¾ cups homemade beef broth
1 can (1 lb.) red kidney beans
½ cup dry red wine
Salt (optional)
Shredded Parmesan cheese

1. Remove casings and crumble Italian sausage into a 3 to 4-quart saucepan. Cook, stirring, until sausage browns lightly. Add onion and cook until it begins to brown. Spoon off most of the sausage drippings.

2. Add garlic, green pepper, herb seasoning, tomatoes (coarsely chopped) and their liquid, tomato sauce, broth and kidney beans and their liquid. Bring to boiling, cover, reduce heat and simmer 30 minutes.

3. Stir in wine and cook, uncovered, about 3 minutes. Salt to taste. Serve with Parmesan cheese.

Makes 4 servings.

Short Ribs and Celery Root Soup

Gnarled and knobby, celery root is one of the least glamorous looking of vegetables. But its rich, earthy flavor makes it a mainstay of German soups and boiled dinners. Try it in this beefy soup—the broth is clear and golden, and fresh tomatoes and parsley stirred in just before serving make it glisten and gleam. Serve the soup with hot, buttery garlic bread. If you like, complement the soup with a tart spoonful of yogurt or a squeeze of lemon.

3 pounds beef short ribs
1 tablespoon _each_ butter or margarine and salad oil
1 celery root (about 1½ lbs.), peeled and cut in julienne strips
2 carrots, thinly sliced
1 red bell pepper, seeded and cut in 2-inch-long strips
2 medium onions, thinly sliced and separated into rings
1 large clove garlic, minced or pressed
2 quarts water
1 tablespoon salt
¼ teaspoon white pepper
1 bay leaf
½ teaspoon crumbled thyme
1 tomato, peeled and finely chopped
½ cup chopped parsley
Plain, unflavored yogurt, _or_ lemon wedges (optional)

1. In a 5 to 6-quart kettle or Dutch oven, brown short ribs well on all sides in heated butter and oil. Spoon off drippings. Add celery root, carrots, red pepper, onions, garlic, water, salt, white pepper, bay leaf and thyme. Bring to boiling, cover and simmer for 3 to 4 hours, until meat is very tender and broth is richly flavored.

2. Using a slotted spoon, remove short ribs. When cool enough to handle, remove meat from bones and return it to soup in chunks. Discard bones and fat. (If possible, cover and chill soup for several hours or overnight.)

3. Skim and reheat soup to serving temperature. Salt to taste. Stir in tomato and parsley. Serve with yogurt or lemon wedges to add at the table.

Makes 4 to 6 servings.

Short ribs, celery root for hearty soup.

Easy Eggplant Soup

For short-notice meals, it's a good idea to have a few quick-cooking soups in your culinary repertoire. One that is notable is this tomatoey vegetable soup; it begins with a pound of ground beef and is ready to serve in less than an hour.

1 pound ground beef, crumbled
1 large onion, chopped
1 tablespoon _each_ butter or margarine and olive oil or salad oil
1 large clove garlic, minced or pressed
1 medium eggplant (about 1½ lbs.), cut in ¾-inch cubes (unpeeled)
2 medium carrots, shredded
1 green pepper, seeded and cut in 2-inch-long strips
1 large can (28 oz.) tomatoes
1 teaspoon _each_ salt, sugar and dried basil
½ teaspoon ground nutmeg
¼ teaspoon pepper
2 cans (13¾ oz. _each_) regular-strength beef broth, _or_ 3½ cups homemade beef broth
½ cup chopped parsley
Shredded Parmesan cheese

1. Brown beef and onion in heated butter and oil in a 5 to 6-quart Dutch oven. Add garlic, eggplant, carrots and green pepper and cook, stirring occasionally, until eggplant browns lightly.

2. Stir in tomatoes (coarsely chopped) and their liquid, salt, sugar, basil, nutmeg, pepper and broth. Bring to boiling, reduce heat, cover and simmer for 45 to 50 minutes, until the eggplant is very tender.

3. Stir in parsley. Salt to taste. Serve with cheese at the table.

Makes 4 to 6 servings.

For a quick family supper, serve a hearty pot of eggplant soup with ground beef, vegetables and shredded Parmesan cheese.

Lamb meatballs, zucchini and lemon combine in a sparkling Greek soup. Accompany it with braided egg bread.

Meatball and Ravioli Soup

So substantial it can almost be eaten with a fork, this soup needs only green salad and red jug wine.

    Meatballs (recipe follows)
1 tablespoon olive oil or
    salad oil
1 large onion, finely chopped
1 clove garlic, minced or pressed
1 large can (28 oz.) tomatoes
¼ cup tomato paste
1 can (13¾ oz.) regular-strength
    beef broth, *or* 1¾ cups
    homemade beef broth
½ cup dry red wine
1 cup water
½ teaspoon *each* sugar and
    crumbled basil
¼ teaspoon *each* crumbled thyme
    and oregano
1 package (12 oz.) frozen ravioli
    (plain, without sauce), thawed
¼ cup chopped parsley
    Grated Parmesan cheese

1. In a 4 to 6-quart Dutch oven brown meatballs carefully in heated oil. Mix in onion and garlic and cook about 5 minutes, taking care not to break up meatballs. Add tomatoes (coarsely chopped) and their liquid, tomato paste, broth, wine, water, sugar, basil, thyme and oregano. Bring to boiling, reduce heat, cover and simmer 30 minutes.

2. Add ravioli and cook, covered, at a gentle boil for as long as specified on ravioli package (10 to 15 minutes), until ravioli are just tender and no longer taste starchy. Salt to taste. Stir in parsley. Serve with cheese to sprinkle over the thick soup.

Makes 4 to 6 servings.

Meatballs: Lightly beat 1 egg; mix in ¼ cup *each* soft bread crumbs and grated Parmesan cheese, ¾ teaspoon onion salt, 1 clove garlic (minced or pressed) and 1 pound ground lean beef. Shape into 1-inch balls.

Greek Meatball and Zucchini Soup

Exceptionally simple and speedy to put together, this soup is given character by meatballs of ground lamb accented with fresh lemon. It is especially good when made with homemade chicken stock (see page 11). Accompany the soup with a loaf of braided egg bread.

    Lamb Meatballs (recipe follows)
1½ tablespoons olive oil or salad oil
1 large onion, finely chopped
½ teaspoon crumbled oregano
2 cans (13¾ oz. *each*), *or* 3½ to 4
    cups homemade regular-
    strength chicken broth
2 tablespoons long grain rice
2 medium zucchini (about ¾ lb.),
    thinly sliced
    Salt (optional)
    Lemon wedges

1. Brown meatballs on all sides in heated oil in a 4 to 6-quart Dutch oven. Add onion, oregano, broth and rice. Bring to boiling, cover, reduce heat and simmer for about 25 minutes, until rice is tender.

2. Add zucchini and cook, uncovered, until zucchini is just tender, 4 to 6 minutes. Salt to taste, and serve. Pass lemon wedges to squeeze into individual servings.

Makes 4 servings.

Lamb Meatballs: In a mixing bowl, beat 1 egg. Mix in 1 teaspoon salt, 1 clove garlic (minced or pressed), dash pepper and ¼ cup soft bread crumbs. Lightly mix in 1 pound ground lamb. Shape into ¾-inch meatballs.

Green Split Pea Soup with Ham Hocks

Here is a soup for a cold, rainy day, when its robust flavor and nourishing substance can be counted on to warm one's very bones. Accompany it with corn muffins and, for dessert, spicy baked apples.

3 to 4 small smoked ham hocks (2 to 2½ lbs.)
3 quarts water
2 medium onions, chopped
2 stalks celery, chopped (include leaves)
1 teaspoon crumbled tarragon
½ cup chopped parsley
⅛ teaspoon *each* nutmeg and white pepper
1 pound green split peas, rinsed and drained
1 tablespoon lemon juice
Salt

1. Place ham hocks in a 6 to 8-quart kettle with water, onions, celery and tarragon. Bring to boiling, reduce heat, cover and simmer for 3 to 4 hours, until meat is very tender. Remove ham hocks and, when cool enough to handle, discard bones and skin. Return meat to broth in large chunks.

2. Add parsley, nutmeg, pepper and split peas. Simmer, uncovered, for 1½ to 2 hours longer, stirring occasionally. If possible, refrigerate the soup several hours or overnight. Skim off fat and reheat the soup over medium heat to serving temperature, stirring occasionally. Stir in lemon juice. Add salt to taste.

Makes 6 to 8 servings.

Chili Bean Soup

If your family likes chili, this red bean soup with chunks of pork is sure to please. Accompany it with a green salad and tortilla chips for a hearty, Mexican accented meal.

1 pound dried red beans, rinsed and drained
7 cups water
1 tablespoon salad oil
2 pounds country-style spareribs
1 green pepper, seeded and chopped
2 medium onions, sliced
2 cloves garlic, minced or pressed
2 teaspoons salt
2 tablespoons chili powder
½ teaspoon ground cumin
1 can (8 oz.) tomato sauce
Shredded Monterey jack cheese

1. Place beans in a large bowl; add 4 cups of the water and let stand overnight (or, if you prefer, bring beans and 4 cups water to a boil in a 4-quart kettle, boil briskly for 2 minutes, then remove from heat and let stand, covered, for 1 hour).

2. Heat oil in a 5 to 6-quart Dutch oven or deep kettle. In it brown spareribs well on all sides. Add green pepper, onions and garlic; brown lightly. Mix in remaining 3 cups water, bring to boiling, reduce heat, cover and simmer for 1½ to 2 hours, until meat is tender.

3. Remove spareribs from pan, remove meat from bones and return to the cooking liquid in chunks, discarding bones and fat. (At this point, you may refrigerate overnight, then skim off fat and reheat.)

4. Mix in soaked beans and their liquid, salt, chili powder and cumin; bring to boiling. Cover, reduce heat and simmer for 1½ hours, until beans are almost tender. Mix in tomato sauce. Cook for about 1 hour longer, until beans are very tender. Serve sprinkled with cheese.

Makes 6 to 8 servings.

Ruth's Barley and White Bean Soup

Somewhat lighter than many bean soups, this one has chewy, nutlike kernels of plump barley in a full-flavored vegetable broth.

½ cup small white beans, rinsed and drained
2 quarts water
2 tablespoons butter or margarine
1 small onion, finely chopped
2 leeks, well rinsed and thinly sliced
⅓ cup pearl barley
1 clove garlic, minced or pressed
1 stalk celery, finely chopped
1 medium carrot, shredded
2 smoked ham hocks (1½ to 2 lbs.), *or* 1 meaty ham bone
1 bay leaf
⅛ teaspoon white pepper
1 cup milk
Salt (optional)
Chopped parsley or snipped chives

1. Bring beans and 2 cups of the water to boiling; boil for 2 minutes. Remove from heat, cover and let stand for 1 hour.

2. In a 5½ to 6-quart kettle or Dutch oven, heat butter. In it cook onion, leeks and barley until onion is transparent. Stir in garlic, celery and carrot and cook 2 to 3 minutes. Add ham hocks or bone, remaining 6 cups water, beans and their liquid, bay leaf and pepper.

3. Bring to boiling, cover, reduce heat, and simmer for 2½ to 3 hours, until meat separates easily from bone. Remove ham hocks or ham bone and, when cool enough to handle, remove and discard bones and skin. Discard bay leaf. Return meat in chunks to the soup.

4. Gradually stir in milk and reheat to serving temperature (do not boil). Salt to taste. Sprinkle each portion with parsley or chives, and serve.

Makes 6 servings.

Swedish Yellow Split Pea Soup

If ever a soup could be called beautiful, it is this one—golden yellow, flecked with the orange of carrots and the deep rose of simmered ham.

1 tablespoon butter or margarine
1 medium onion, finely chopped
2 medium carrots, thinly sliced
1 stalk celery, thinly sliced
2 smoked ham hocks (1½ to 2 lbs.), *or* 1 meaty ham bone
1 pound yellow split peas, rinsed and drained
1 can (12 oz.) beer
6 cups water
1 whole cardamom pod, crushed
¼ teaspoon crumbled marjoram
Dash cayenne
1 tablespoon cider vinegar
Salt (optional)

1. In a 5½ to 6-quart kettle or Dutch oven, melt butter. In it cook onion, carrots and celery, stirring occasionally, until onion is soft but not browned. Add ham hocks or bone, peas, beer, water, cardamom, marjoram and cayenne. Bring to boiling, cover, reduce heat and simmer for 2½ to 3 hours, until ham and peas are tender.

2. Remove ham hocks or bone and, when cool enough to handle, remove and discard bones and skin. Return meat to soup in chunks. Stir in vinegar. Salt to taste and reheat to serving temperature.

Makes 6 servings.

Salt Swedish yellow split pea soup to taste.

Dilled Lamb and Barley Soup

Here is a very substantial lamb soup that tastes good with cole slaw made from red cabbage, a dark rye bread and a lemon dessert.

⅔ cup pearl barley
    Water
2 tablespoons butter or margarine
4 lamb shanks (about 3 lbs.)
2 onions, finely chopped
2 cloves garlic, minced or pressed
2 stalks celery, thinly sliced
2 carrots, sliced about ⅛-inch thick
6 cups water
¼ cup chopped parsley
2 teaspoons salt
1 bay leaf
⅛ teaspoon white pepper
1 teaspoon dill weed
    Sour cream

1. Soak barley in water to cover while lamb shanks cook. Heat butter in a 5 to 6-quart Dutch oven or deep kettle. In it brown lamb shanks well on all sides. Mix in onions, garlic, celery and carrots. Then add water, parsley and seasonings. Bring to boiling, cover, and simmer slowly for 2½ to 3 hours, until lamb is very tender.

2. Remove lamb shanks from the soup, then remove meat from the bones, discarding bones, fat and skin. Return meat in pieces to the soup. Discard bay leaf. (At this point, you may chill soup and let barley stand overnight, then skim off fat.)

3. Drain soaked barley and add it to the soup. Bring again to boiling, then cook, covered, until barley is tender, 45 minutes to 1 hour. Salt to taste. Spoon sour cream on each serving.

Makes 6 servings.

Spanish Garbanzo and Spinach Soup

Try dried garbanzo beans (also known as chickpeas and ceci beans) for variety. This legume makes a soup as delicious and hearty as do dried peas and red, brown or black beans.

1 pound dried garbanzo beans, rinsed and drained
2 quarts water
2 tablespoons olive oil or salad oil
1 large onion, finely chopped
1 stalk celery, thinly sliced
2 cloves garlic, minced or pressed
2 cups ½-inch-wide strips smoked pork shoulder picnic, or ham
1 bay leaf
1 small dried red chile pepper, crushed
½ teaspoon crumbled thyme
1 can (1 lb.) tomatoes
1 bunch (8 to 10 oz.) fresh spinach
    Salt
1 hard-cooked egg, pressed through a sieve

1. Place beans in a large bowl, add water, and let stand overnight (or, if you prefer, bring beans and water to boiling in a 4-quart kettle, boil briskly for 2 minutes, then remove from heat and let stand, covered, for 1 hour).

2. Heat oil in a 5½ to 6-quart kettle or Dutch oven. In it cook onion, celery, garlic and ham strips until vegetables are soft. Add beans and their liquid, bay leaf, red pepper and thyme. Bring to boiling, cover, reduce heat and simmer for 1 hour. Add tomatoes (coarsely chopped) and their liquid and continue cooking until beans are tender, about 2 hours longer.

3. Meanwhile, rinse and drain spinach well, remove and discard stems, and chop leaves coarsely. Stir spinach into soup and continue cooking, uncovered, about 5 minutes. Salt to taste.

4. Serve in broad shallow bowls, sprinkled with sieved hard-cooked egg.

Makes 6 servings.

Velvety Chicken and Mushroom Soup

Here is a creamy, rich chicken soup with elegance and finesse. If you wish, you can prepare it ahead through step 2. Wait to add the cream, chicken and the lemon-egg mixture until just before you are ready to serve it.

    Chicken Breasts and Broth (recipe follows)
½ pound mushrooms, sliced
2 tablespoons butter or margarine
1 small onion, finely chopped
1½ tablespoons flour
⅛ teaspoon crumbled thyme
    Dash of white pepper
1 teaspoon catsup
1 cup half-and-half (light cream)
1 egg, slightly beaten
1 tablespoon lemon juice
    Salt

1. Prepare chicken and broth according to directions; set meat and broth aside separately.

2. In a 3-quart saucepan, cook sliced mushrooms in heated butter until lightly browned; set aside about ¼ cup of the mushrooms for garnish. To remaining mushrooms in pan, add onion, cooking and stirring until limp but not browned. Mix in flour until bubbly. Add thyme, pepper and catsup. Remove from heat and gradually mix in broth. Cook, stirring, until soup boils gently. Cover and simmer 15 minutes. Whirl until smooth in blender; return soup to cooking pan.

3. Stir in half-and-half and chicken; cook until soup is steaming hot. Beat egg with lemon juice. Stir in a little of the hot soup. Pour egg mixture into hot soup. Cook, stirring, until very hot but not boiling. Salt to taste.

Stir in reserved mushrooms. Serve the soup steaming hot.

Makes 3 to 4 servings.

Chicken Breasts and Broth: In a 2½ to 3-quart saucepan combine 3 half chicken breasts (about 1½ lbs.), 1 stalk celery (thinly sliced), 1 medium onion (chopped), 1 teaspoon salt, 2 whole allspice and 2½ cups water. Bring to boiling, cover, reduce heat and simmer 45 minutes. Pour through a colander, reserving broth. Discard seasonings, bones and skin. Break or cut the chicken into generous bite-size pieces.

Chicken and Escarole Soup

This is a main dish version of an Italian soup that is generally served as a first course. With the addition of a generous quantity of chicken, accompanied by bread sticks and vegetable relishes, it easily becomes a hearty meal.

3½ to 4-pound frying chicken, cut up
1 large onion, finely chopped
1 small carrot, thinly sliced
1 sprig parsley
1 bay leaf
1 stalk celery, chopped (include leaves)
2 teaspoons salt
⅛ teaspoon *each* nutmeg and white pepper
¼ teaspoon crumbled thyme
1 quart water
¼ cup tiny shell macaroni
2 cups thinly sliced inner leaves escarole
2 tablespoons butter or margarine
    Grated Parmesan cheese

1. In a 4 to 6-quart kettle or Dutch oven combine chicken pieces, onion, carrot, parsley, bay leaf, celery, salt, nutmeg, pepper, thyme and water. Bring to boiling, reduce heat, cover and simmer for about 2 hours, until chicken is very tender. Strain broth, remove and discard skin and bones. Return chicken to broth in large pieces, discarding vegetables and whole seasonings. (This much can be prepared ahead, if you wish, and later reheated.)

2. Reheat soup to a gentle boil, add macaroni and cook, uncovered, until just tender (see package directions for cooking time).

3. Meanwhile, cook escarole in heated butter in a medium frying pan, stirring until it is wilted and bright green, about 3 minutes. Stir escarole mixture into soup. Salt to taste. Serve in broad soup bowls; pass Parmesan cheese.

Makes 4 servings.

Chicken aplenty and a rich broth make a main dish of a classic Italian soup.

Tips for Freezing Soups

Few kinds of cooked dishes freeze as well as soups. Serious cooks use their freezers at several stages of the soup-making process:

☐ Freeze bones until you are ready to make broth or soup.

☐ Freeze beef or chicken broth or beef concentrate (see pages 10 and 11) to have available for other dishes.

☐ Freeze completed soups in family or single serving portions.

You can freeze soups in plastic or coated cardboard freezer containers, in coffee or shortening cans, or in large glass jars. Be sure to leave at least an inch at the top to allow for expansion of the liquid as it freezes.

Frozen soups should be used within four months, so it is a good idea to label soups with a date.

Most frozen soups can be heated over direct low heat, stirring frequently. Soups containing milk should be reheated in a double boiler.

Soups thickened with eggs, such as the Velvety Chicken and Mushroom Soup (page 52) and Flemish Chicken Soup (on this page), will be best if you wait to add the egg mixture after the frozen soup is thawed and reheated.

When a recipe specifies adding some of the fresh vegetables at the very end of the cooking time to enhance their color and texture, omit them from the soup if you plan to make it ahead and freeze it. (See Milanese Vegetable-Beef Soup, page 45, and Short Ribs and Celery Root Soup, page 48.) When you reheat the soup, add the vegetables as directed in the original recipes.

Flemish Chicken Soup

A plump stewing chicken gives this Belgian soup a rich flavor, which is accented by egg yolks, cream and lemon juice. You might accompany it with an endive salad with a mustard dressing, a coarse-textured whole wheat bread and sweet butter.

3 tablespoons butter or margarine
2 stalks celery, thinly sliced
2 leeks, well rinsed and thinly sliced (white and pale green parts only)
2 medium onions, thinly sliced and separated into rings
4 to 5-pound stewing hen, cut up
6 cups water
1 cup dry white wine
2 teaspoons salt
2 sprigs parsley
½ bay leaf
½ teaspoon crumbled thyme
⅛ teaspoon *each* nutmeg and white pepper
Juice of 1 lemon
3 egg yolks
½ cup whipping cream
Lemon slices, for garnish

1. Melt butter in a deep 6 to 8-quart kettle or Dutch oven. Add celery, leeks and onions. Cook, stirring, until soft but not browned. Add chicken pieces, water, wine, salt, parsley, bay leaf, thyme, nutmeg and white pepper. Bring to boiling, reduce heat, cover and simmer for about 2 hours, until chicken is very tender.

2. With a slotted spoon, remove chicken pieces. Discard bones and skin. Place chicken, in good size chunks, in a warm soup tureen. Ladle

Elegant Flemish soup starts with chicken.

on a little of the cooking liquid; cover and keep warm in a 250° oven until ready to serve.

3. Remove and discard bay leaf and parsley from the broth. Mix lemon juice into broth. In a bowl, beat egg yolks with cream until well blended. Gradually pour in about 1 cup of the hot broth, stirring constantly. Stir egg yolk mixture into broth. Cook over low heat, stirring constantly with a wire whisk, until steaming hot (do not boil). Salt to taste. Pour broth over chicken in tureen. Garnish with lemon slices.

Makes 6 servings.

Goodbye-to-the-Thanksgiving-Turkey Soup

As good tasting as it is economical, this soup is made with the very last of a festive turkey. Into the kettle go the turkey carcass and any available large bones. Enhance the flavor, if need be, by adding canned or homemade chicken broth toward the end of the cooking process.

Meaty turkey carcass and large bones
2 carrots, thinly sliced
1 stalk celery, sliced
1 onion, cut in eighths
1 bay leaf
2 sprigs parsley
⅛ teaspoon *each* nutmeg and crumbled thyme
1 teaspoon salt
½ teaspoon whole white or black peppers
3 quarts water
½ cup thinly sliced celery
2 to 4 cups chicken broth (if needed)
½ cup tiny shell macaroni
¼ cup frozen peas, thawed

1. Break up turkey carcass and place bones in a 5 to 6-quart Dutch oven or deep kettle. Add one of the carrots, the stalk of celery, onion, seasonings and water. Bring to boiling, then reduce heat and simmer, covered, 3 hours. Uncover and simmer 1 hour longer to reduce liquid.

2. Strain into large bowl. Discard bones and vegetables, returning any meat to the broth. (At this point, soup may be refrigerated, then skimmed.)

3. Return soup to the cooking pot. Add the second carrot, sliced celery and additional broth if needed to enhance flavor. Bring to boiling again, reduce heat and simmer, covered, until carrots and celery are tender, about 1 hour.

4. Add macaroni and cook at a gentle boil until nearly tender—about 10 minutes. Stir in peas and continue cooking about 3 minutes. Salt to taste.

Makes 4 to 6 servings.

A friendly party centers around a tureen of Swiss Ham and Potato Soup.

Soup suppers for family and friends

An informal gathering around a soup tureen is one of the warmest and friendliest meals imaginable. Here are some ideas for menus featuring great soup recipes. Recipes for some of the suggested accompaniments—first courses, breads, desserts and wine or beverage ideas—follow. You might set up these soup suppers as buffets for serving ease. Keep the soup hot on an electric serving tray, in a chafing dish or on a hotplate.

Swiss Potato Soup Supper

This rich and creamy soup is made with potatoes and bits of smoky ham. At the table, sprinkle each portion with shredded Swiss cheese to melt and add a sweet, nutlike flavor.

**Crisp Raw Vegetables:
Cherry Tomatoes, Green Onions,
Carrot and Cucumber Sticks,
Cauliflower
Swiss Ham and Potato Soup
Warm French Bread   Butter
Fresh Lemon Bars
Suggested wine: Alsatian Sylvaner
or Riesling**

Swiss Ham and Potato Soup

**4 large boiling potatoes (about 2
    lbs.), peeled and sliced to make
    about 5 cups
3 cups water
1 teaspoon salt
¼ teaspoon crumbled thyme
6 green onions
3 tablespoons butter or margarine
1½ cups diced smoked pork
    shoulder picnic, or ham
2 tablespoons flour
1 teaspoon Dijon-style mustard
⅛ teaspoon *each* white pepper and
    nutmeg
3 cups milk
1 cup shredded Swiss cheese**

1. Place potatoes in a 4 to 6-quart saucepan and add water, salt, thyme and the white part only of 3 of the green onions, thinly sliced. Bring to boiling, reduce heat and boil gently, uncovered, for 20 to 25 minutes, until potatoes are very tender. Remove from heat and mash with a potato masher until creamy.

2. Meanwhile, melt butter in a 2-quart saucepan. In it, cook ham until lightly browned. Blend in flour, mustard, pepper and nutmeg; cook until bubbly. Remove from heat and gradually pour in milk, stirring constantly. Return to heat and cook, stirring constantly, until sauce is thickened.

3. Mix ham sauce smoothly into potatoes. Slice remaining 3 onions (includ-ing green tops), and mix into soup. Reheat to serving temperature. Salt to taste. Serve with shredded cheese to sprinkle and melt over each portion.

Makes 4 to 6 servings.

Fresh Lemon Bars

**1 cup (½ lb.) soft butter or
    margarine
½ cup powdered sugar
1 teaspoon vanilla
2 cups unsifted all-purpose flour
4 eggs
2 cups granulated sugar
    Grated rind of 1 lemon
6 tablespoons lemon juice
    Powdered sugar**

1. Cream butter, the ½ cup powdered sugar and vanilla until fluffy; mix in flour until well blended. Spread evenly in a well buttered 13 by 9-inch baking pan. Bake in a 350° oven for 20 minutes.

2. Meanwhile, in a bowl stir until com-bined (do not beat) eggs, granulated sugar, lemon rind and lemon juice. Pour egg mixture over baked layer. Continue baking for 18 to 22 minutes longer, until topping is set and lightly browned.

3. While cookies are still warm, sift with additional powdered sugar to cover top generously. Cut into bars. Cool before serving.

Makes 36 bars.

Hungarian Goulash Soup Supper

Goulash or *gulyás* takes many forms in Hungary, one of which is a hefty soup made with red bell peppers and seasoned with caraway seed, paprika and garlic. Accompany it with dark rye bread and a red wine such as California Zinfandel.

**Butter Lettuce Salad   Tart Dressing
Hungarian Goulash Soup
Dark Rye Bread   Sweet Butter
Green Apple Torte
Suggested wine: California Zinfandel**

Hungarian Goulash Soup

**3 pounds boneless English-cut short ribs, cut in about 1½-inch chunks
2 tablespoons *each* salad oil and butter or margarine
2 large onions, chopped
1 clove garlic, mashed
1 tablespoon paprika
5 cups water
1 large red bell pepper, seeded and cut in thin strips
2 teaspoons salt
⅛ teaspoon white pepper
1 teaspoon caraway seed
2 tomatoes, peeled and coarsely chopped
1 small dried hot red chile pepper, crushed
2 medium potatoes, cut lengthwise in eighths
Sour cream**

1. Brown meat, about a fourth at a time, in heated oil in a 4½ to 5-quart Dutch oven; remove and reserve meat as it browns. When all the meat is browned, pour off pan drippings and discard them. Melt butter in the same pan. Add onions and garlic, and cook over medium heat until onions are soft and golden; blend in paprika.

2. Stir in browned meat and its juices, water, red pepper strips, salt, white pepper, caraway seed, tomatoes and chile pepper. Bring to boiling, reduce heat, cover and simmer about 2½ hours, until the meat is tender. Cover and refrigerate several hours or overnight.

3. Skim off fat and discard it. Bring soup to a simmer. Add potatoes and cook about 30 minutes longer, until they are tender. Taste and add salt, if needed. Pass sour cream to spoon on at the table.

Makes 6 to 8 servings.

Sour cream is spooned over servings of goulash soup to each diner's taste.

Green Apple Torte

**8 medium-size tart green apples, peeled, cored and sliced
2 tablespoons butter or margarine
¾ cup sugar
Vanilla Wafer Crust (recipe follows)
7 eggs
2 cups sour cream
¼ teaspoon nutmeg
1 teaspoon vanilla**

1. In a large frying pan, stir apple slices in melted butter; lightly blend in sugar. Cook, stirring occasionally, over medium heat until apples begin to soften, 6 to 8 minutes. Remove apple mixture from heat.

2. Remove and reserve ½ cup of the crust mixture. Press remainder evenly over bottom and 2 inches up the sides of a well buttered 9-inch springform pan with a removable bottom.

3. Beat eggs with sour cream and nutmeg until well combined; lightly blend in vanilla and apple mixture. Pour into crust-lined pan. Bake in a 350° oven for 30 minutes; sprinkle with remaining crust mixture. Continue baking 15 to 20 minutes longer, until filling is set. Chill until ready to serve, several hours or overnight. Remove pan sides before serving on pan bottom.

Makes 10 to 12 servings.

Vanilla Wafer Crust: With a rolling pin, or in blender, crush enough packaged vanilla wafers to make 1¼ cups fine crumbs. Mix with ¼ cup sugar and ¾ teaspoon cinnamon; into the mixture cut ¼ cup butter or margarine until fine crumbs are formed.

Tart Green Apple Torte can be prepared ahead.

Oxtail Soup Supper

Thick, rich oxtail soup suggests a German menu. Start the meal with a tangy first course of herring and beets in a creamy dressing, arranged on lettuce leaves. Accompany the soup with a wonderful homemade rye bread, served slightly warm in thick slices. Following such a sturdy repast, a bowl of fresh seasonal citrus fruits, crisp apples and nuts is in order for a help-yourself dessert.

Beet and Herring Salad
Sherried Oxtail Soup
Buttermilk Rye Bread   Butter
Fresh Fruit Bowl:
Tangerines, Apples, Nuts in Shells
Suggested beverage: Beer

Beet and Herring Salad

1 large jar (12 oz.) herring fillets in wine sauce
1 can (16 oz.) julienne-style beets, well drained
½ cup thinly sliced celery
⅓ cup *each* mayonnaise and sour cream
   Butter or leaf lettuce
   Snipped chives
2 hard-cooked eggs, sliced

1. Drain liquid from herring. Discard bay leaf and whole peppers from mixture. Cut herring in bite-size pieces. Lightly combine herring, beets and celery with mixture of mayonnaise and sour cream. Cover and chill for several hours to blend flavors.

2. Serve herring mixture on lettuce leaves. Sprinkle the salad with chives and garnish with slices of hard-cooked eggs.

Makes 6 servings.

Sherried Oxtail Soup

3 pounds oxtails, cut into segments
   Salt, white pepper, ground allspice and flour
2 tablespoons butter or margarine
3 onions, chopped
3 carrots, shredded
1 small rutabaga (about ½ lb.), peeled and sliced
1 small celery root (about 12 oz.), peeled and cubed
5 cups water
1 teaspoon *each* salt and paprika
⅛ teaspoon *each* white pepper, cayenne and crumbled thyme
1 bay leaf
½ cup dry sherry

1. Sprinkle oxtails lightly with salt, pepper and allspice, then coat lightly with flour. In a 5 to 6-quart kettle or Dutch oven, brown oxtails well on all sides in heated butter, removing oxtails as they brown. When all are browned, pour off most of the pan drippings. Add onions and carrots; cook, stirring occasionally, until limp and lightly browned. Return oxtails to pan with rutabaga, celery root, water and seasonings (except sherry). Bring to boiling, reduce heat, cover and simmer for about 4 hours, until meat is very tender.

2. Skim off fat, then strain the soup to separate out the meat and vegetables. Return the liquid to the kettle. Discard bay leaf. Remove meat from bones; add meat to broth. Place strained vegetables in blender with a little of the broth; whirl until smooth. Mix puréed vegetables into broth.

3. Boil soup gently, uncovered, for about 20 minutes to reduce liquid slightly. Stir in the sherry. Add salt to taste.

Makes 4 to 6 servings.

Buttermilk Rye Bread

1 envelope active dry yeast
1 tablespoon honey
1 cup warm water
3½ cups unsifted all-purpose flour (approximately)
2 cups buttermilk
1 tablespoon salt
1 cup graham flour or whole wheat flour
2½ cups rye flour
1 egg white, slightly beaten with 1 teaspoon water
1 tablespoon poppy seeds

1. In the large bowl of an electric mixer, stir together yeast, honey and water. Stir in 1 cup of the all-purpose flour. Let stand in a warm place until bubbly, 20 to 25 minutes.

2. Mix buttermilk and salt into the risen mixture. Add 2 cups more all-purpose flour, mix to blend, then beat with mixer at medium speed for 5 minutes. Stir in graham and rye flours, about 1 cup at a time, to make a stiff dough. Turn out on a floured board or pastry cloth and knead until dough is smooth and springy, kneading in up to ½ cup more all-purpose flour, if necessary. Place dough in a greased bowl, cover lightly, and let rise until doubled, about 1¼ hours.

3. Punch dough down, let rest 5 minutes, then divide in half. Shape each half into a loaf and place in a greased 9 by 5-inch loaf pan. Let rise again until doubled, about 45 minutes. Brush lightly with egg white mixture; sprinkle with poppy seeds. Bake in a 350° oven for 40 to 45 minutes, until loaves are well browned and sound hollow when tapped lightly.

Makes 2 loaves.

Turkey Drumsticks and Barley Soup Supper

Turkey is now quite readily available already cut into parts, and drumsticks are one of the most economical forms in which to buy it. From two or three large drumsticks, you can make this rich and delicious soup.

Turkey Drumsticks and Barley Soup
Spicy Pumpkin Muffins   Butter
Molded Citrus Salad
Date and Walnut Brownies
Vanilla Ice Cream
Suggested wine: Jug Chablis

Spicy Pumpkin Muffins

1½ cups unsifted all-purpose flour
½ cup sugar
2 teaspoons baking powder
¾ teaspoon salt
1 teaspoon cinnamon
½ teaspoon ground ginger
¼ teaspoon ground cloves
½ cup raisins
1 egg
½ cup *each* milk and canned pumpkin
¼ cup salad oil
2½ teaspoons sugar, mixed with ½ teaspoon cinnamon

1. In a mixing bowl stir together flour, sugar, baking powder, salt and spices until well combined; mix in raisins to coat well with flour mixture. In a smaller bowl, beat egg with milk, pumpkin and oil.

2. Stir egg mixture, all at once, into flour mixture, mixing only until combined. Fill greased or nonstick muffin pans two-thirds full; sprinkle with sugar and cinnamon mixture. Bake in a 400° oven for 20 to 25 minutes, until nicely browned. Serve warm.

Makes 12 muffins.

Top Date and Walnut Brownies with ice cream.

Savory Turkey and Barley Soup is accompanied by warm pumpkin muffins and a molded salad.

Turkey Drumsticks and Barley Soup

  2 to 3 turkey drumsticks (2½ to 3 lbs.)
  2 tablespoons butter or margarine
  1 large onion, finely chopped
  3 stalks celery, thinly sliced
  2 large carrots, sliced
  1 clove garlic, minced or pressed
  ¼ teaspoon poultry seasoning
  1½ teaspoons seasoned salt
  6 cups water
  1 cup dry white wine
  ¼ cup pearl barley
  Salt (optional)
  ¼ cup finely chopped parsley

1. In a broad 5½ to 6-quart kettle or Dutch oven, brown turkey drumsticks well on all sides in heated butter. Add onion, celery, carrots, garlic, poultry seasoning, seasoned salt, water, wine and barley. Bring to boiling, cover, re- duce heat and simmer for 2½ to 3 hours, until turkey is very tender.

2. Remove turkey from soup and, when cool enough to handle, discard bones, tendons and skin. Return tur- key in chunks to soup. Salt to taste. Reheat to serving temperature, stir in parsley and serve very hot.

Makes 4 to 6 servings.

Date and Walnut Brownies

  ⅔ cup unsifted all-purpose flour
  ½ teaspoon baking powder
  ⅓ cup butter or margarine
  2 squares (2 oz.) unsweetened chocolate
  1 cup sugar
  2 eggs
  1 teaspoon vanilla
  ⅓ cup *each* chopped walnuts and snipped dates

1. Sift flour with baking powder. In a small heavy saucepan over low heat, slowly melt butter with chocolate; cool slightly. In a mixing bowl, gradually add sugar to eggs, beating until smooth and well combined. Blend in chocolate mixture and vanilla. Add flour mixture; mix well. Stir in walnuts and dates.

2. Spread batter evenly in a greased or nonstick, 8-inch square baking pan. Bake in a 350° oven for about 25 minutes, until edges begin to pull away from pan sides and a wooden pick comes out clean when it is in- serted near the center.

3. Place pan on a wire rack to cool for 20 to 30 minutes; cut into 2-inch squares. Brownies are at their best served slightly warm topped with vanilla ice cream or whipped cream.

Makes 16 brownies.

Lamb Borsch Supper

Colorful borsch is the focus of this soup supper for 6 to 8. Precede it with a tangy eggplant spread, a sort of poor man's caviar. The ruby-colored Russian soup can be made from bones saved from lamb shoulder roasts or with savory inexpensive lamb neck bones.

A light fruity Beaujolais from France or a California Gamay Beaujolais is a pleasing complement to the soup. With the crumbly almond topped cherry pie for dessert, pour milk or full-bodied after-dinner coffee.

Eggplant Caviar   Rye Melba Toast
Lamb Bone Borsch
Cherry Streusel Pie
Suggested wine: Beaujolais

Eggplant Caviar

- **2 small eggplants (about 1 pound *each*), unpeeled**
- **1 large onion, finely chopped**
- **6 tablespoons olive oil**
- **3 cloves garlic, minced or pressed**
- **⅓ cup catsup**
- **½ cup chopped parsley**
- **2 tablespoons drained capers**
- **1½ teaspoons salt**
- **½ teaspoon pepper**
- **¼ teaspoon cinnamon**
- **1 tablespoon *each* dried mint, grated lemon rind and lemon juice**
- **2 tablespoons red wine vinegar Melba toast**

1. Cut eggplants in halves lengthwise; place cut side down in an oiled baking pan. Bake uncovered in a 350° oven until eggplant is very tender, from 50 to 60 minutes.

2. Meanwhile, sauté onion in heated oil in a 1½-quart saucepan, stirring occasionally, until lightly browned. Stir in garlic and catsup. Simmer, uncovered, for 15 minutes.

3. When eggplant is tender, scoop out the meat and discard peel. Mash coarsely in a bowl. Stir in onion mixture, parsley, capers, salt, pepper, cinnamon, mint, lemon rind, lemon juice and vinegar. Cover and chill to blend flavors for several hours or overnight. Serve as a spread on Melba toast.

Makes about 3½ cups.

Precede hearty supper featuring lamb borsch with an eggplant spread for crisp rye toast. For dessert serve crumble-top cherry pie with milk or demi-tasse coffee.

Lamb Bone Borsch

- **5 pounds (about) meaty lamb bones**
- **3 quarts water**
- **1 tablespoon salt**
- **¼ teaspoon pepper**
- **1 bay leaf**
- **2 medium onions, sliced**
- **2 stalks celery, thinly sliced (include leaves, chopped)**
- **6 to 8 medium-size beets**
- **2 large carrots, coarsely shredded**
- **1 large boiling potato, diced in ½-inch cubes**
- **1 can (1 lb.) tomatoes**
- **1 small head (about 1 lb.) cabbage**
- **1 tablespoon sugar**
- **2 tablespoons red wine vinegar Sour cream Snipped fresh dill or dried dill weed**

1. In a large soup kettle (at least 8-quart size), combine lamb bones, water, salt, pepper, bay leaf, onions and celery. Bring to boiling, cover, reduce heat and simmer for 1 hour.

2. Meanwhile, cut tops from beets (cook greens separately, as a vegetable) and scrub them. Add whole, unpeeled beets to kettle and continue cooking, covered, 1 hour longer. Remove bones with a slotted spoon and reserve them until they are cool enough to handle. Remove beets, peel and dice them in ½-inch cubes.

3. To soup add cut beets, carrots, potato and tomatoes (coarsely chopped) and their liquid. Remove meat from bones and add it to the soup, discarding bones. Bring soup to boiling and boil gently, uncovered, about 1 hour.

4. If possible, at this point chill soup overnight; skim off fat. Reheat until soup boils gently. Cut cabbage into long thin wedges; remove and discard core. Add cabbage to soup. Continue cooking, uncovered, until cabbage is just tender, about 10 minutes. Stir in sugar and vinegar. Salt to taste. Serve in large bowls with dollops of sour cream sprinkled with dill.

Makes 8 servings.

Cherry Streusel Pie

- **1 package (20 oz.) frozen, unsweetened red sour pitted cherries, thawed**
- **2 tablespoons quick-cooking tapioca**
- **1 cup sugar**
- **⅛ teaspoon salt**
- **¼ teaspoon nutmeg**
- **9-inch unbaked pastry shell Almond Streusel (recipe follows)**

1. Mix cherries and their juices, tapioca, sugar, salt and nutmeg. Let stand for 15 minutes. Spread in pie shell. Spoon streusel mixture evenly over the cherries.

2. Bake in a 375° oven for 45 to 50 minutes, until filling is bubbly all over and topping is well browned. Cool.

Makes 6 to 8 servings.

Almond Streusel: Cut ½ cup (¼ lb.) butter or margarine into a mixture of ½ cup firmly packed brown sugar and ¾ cup unsifted all-purpose flour until mixture is crumbly. Lightly mix in ½ cup slivered blanched almonds.

Stews for Special Meals

Learn one of the secrets of good cooks around the world. Slow cooking brings out a wealth of flavor and tenderness in the humblest meats and poultry.

Some of the best known main dishes around the world are basically stews: the *Sauerbraten* of Germany, *pot au feu* from France and for that matter, the traditional New England boiled dinner. The origins of these dishes are diverse, but all are made with less tender—and therefore less expensive—meats.

Thrifty cooks have long known that certain cuts of meat respond best to such slow moist-heat cooking methods as stewing, braising and fricasseeing. The terms braising and stewing can be used somewhat interchangeably (with stewing generally conceded to involve more cooking liquid than braising). Meat or poultry that is fricasseed is usually not browned first, as are braised and stewed meats.

Cooking meat slowly in liquid is a good way to tenderize it. Because meat protein tends to toughen at high temperatures, meat will be more meltingly tender if the cooking liquid stays below the boiling point. One good cook describes this gentle motion as a tremble, with only an occasional bubble.

Cooking in liquid brings out the full flavor as well as the tenderness, and is also a good medium for adding other tastes in the form of wine, fruit or vegetable juices, herbs and spices and hearty root vegetables.

Few of the world's famous stews are regarded as grand or formal dishes. One theory is that most were created by practical women who had more pressing demands on their time than fussing for hours in the kitchen—so they found main dishes that could be put on to cook unattended while they spent the day at other chores.

A family supper in spring is planned around a tender veal stew with carrots and fresh peas (see page 70). Accompany the main dish with butter-browned new potatoes, French bread, a green salad and milk or white wine to drink.

For today's cooks, such dishes have a similar appeal, whether for family meals or for entertaining.

When you think of meats to use for stew, the tidily cut and wrapped packages of perfect cubes come readily to mind. But is your supermarket meat manager's idea of "stew meat" necessarily the best or even most appropriate choice? Probably not. Cutting up a boneless roast is practically no work at all, yet usually the roast is priced somewhat less per pound than comparable stew meat, cubed and packaged. For example, if a boneless veal shoulder roast costs less per pound than veal stew meat, it can be well worth the few minutes it takes to cube it for a stew. A boneless beef chuck or rump roast is often a very economical choice for stew, also. So it pays to take a good look at the meat counter specials before you pick up that handy package labeled "stew."

There is more than one way to cook a stew. The most obvious is in a big deep pot on top of the range, but you can also use an electric frying pan, your oven or a special cooking utensil such as a fanciful ceramic baker or an electric slow cooker.

A substantial stew, cooked in red wine.

Top-of-the Range Stews

The meats you simmer atop the range can be cooked in a variety of utensils. To hold the cooking heat well, select a tightly covered frying pan or Dutch oven made from a heavy material.

Burgundy Beef Stew

Accompany this flavorful stew, made from the center portion of the chuck roast, with tiny new potatoes cooked in their jackets, French bread and a forthright red jug wine.

- **1½ pounds center section beef chuck, from under blade bone (page 7), fat trimmed, cubed**
- **2 tablespoons butter or margarine**
- **½ cup ½-inch-wide strips smoked pork shoulder picnic or ham**
- **2 medium onions, thinly sliced**
- **1 clove garlic, minced or pressed**
- **1 medium carrot, cut in ½-inch slices**
- **¼ cup chopped parsley**
- **1 bay leaf**
- **½ teaspoon salt**
- **⅛ teaspoon pepper**
- **¼ teaspoon crumbled thyme**
- **1 tablespoon tomato paste**
- **1 cup dry red wine**
- **1 can (4 oz.) mushroom pieces and stems**

1. In a large frying pan, brown beef well (about half at a time) in heated butter; as you finish browning beef, add ham strips to brown.

2. Add onions, garlic, carrot, parsley, bay leaf, salt, pepper, thyme and tomato paste. Stir in wine. Mix in mushrooms and their liquid. Bring to boiling, reduce heat, cover and simmer for about 2 hours until meat is very tender. Remove meat and vegetables to a serving dish, using a slotted spoon; keep warm.

3. Bring cooking liquid to boiling, stirring frequently, and cook until reduced and slightly thickened. Salt to taste. Pour over meat and serve.

Makes 4 to 6 servings.

Pot Au Feu

In just about every Western culture one can find a boiled dinner—which, of course, for best results should be gently simmered, *never* actually boiled. The names and the vegetables used to flavor the pot differ, but the meat involved is usually a brisket of beef. Most briskets today end up as corned beef, so you may have to locate a traditional meat dealer to find this cut at all. But the effort is worth it!

Serve the delicious cooking broth from this classic French dish first, as a clear soup, with warm French bread. Then bring on the sliced beef surrounded by the abundance of vegetables that shared the pot (keep them warm in a low oven while you enjoy the first course). Traditional accompaniments to this homey French main dish are mustard, coarse salt and the tiny sour pickles called *cornichons*.

3½ to 4-pound fresh beef brisket
3 or 4 leeks, well rinsed, with green tops trimmed to about 5 inches
2 turnips, quartered
3 large carrots, quartered lengthwise
3 stalks celery, cut in 3-inch lengths (including leaves, chopped)
5 sprigs parsley
1 tablespoon salt
1 bay leaf
¼ teaspoon *each* whole cloves and allspice and crumbled thyme
1 clove garlic, slivered
1 quart water
6 small new red potatoes (peel a 1-inch strip around center)
¼ pound small whole mushrooms
1 small Savoy or green cabbage (about 1 lb.), cut in 8 wedges
Dijon mustard, coarse salt and *cornichons* (sour pickles)

1. Place meat in a large kettle (at least 8-quart size) with leeks, turnips, carrots, celery, parsley, salt, bay leaf, cloves, allspice, thyme, garlic and water. Bring slowly to boiling, cover, reduce heat, simmer about 3 hours.

2. Add potatoes and mushrooms and continue cooking, covered, about 40 minutes longer until meat is very tender and potatoes are almost cooked. Add cabbage and simmer, uncovered, about 10 minutes. Remove brisket and vegetables to a heatproof platter, and spoon on a little broth to keep them moist. Cover with foil and keep warm in a 250° oven.

3. Strain broth to remove seasonings. Salt to taste. Serve as a first course. Then carve brisket in ¼-inch slices and serve surrounded by vegetables, pass mustard, salt and *cornichons*.

Makes 6 to 8 servings.

Savory Braised Beef Shanks

To many good cooks, a beef shank is a single-portion pot roast. Indeed the two are cooked much the same way. Bones with marrow offer a special bonus in delicate flavor. This dish is splendid with honest-to-goodness mashed potatoes.

4 meaty beef shanks (3 to 3½ lbs.), about 1 inch thick
Salt, pepper and flour
1 tablespoon *each* butter or margarine and salad oil
1 medium onion, finely chopped
2 cloves garlic, minced or pressed
1 tablespoon Dijon-style mustard
1 can (13¾ oz.) regular-strength beef broth, *or* 1¾ cups homemade beef broth
1 cup dry red wine
Chopped parsley, for garnish

1. Lightly sprinkle beef shanks on both sides with salt and pepper; coat with flour, shaking off excess. Brown well in heated butter and oil in a large frying pan.

2. Mix in onion, garlic, mustard, beef broth and wine. Bring to boiling, cover, reduce heat and simmer for 2 to 2½ hours, until meat is very tender.

3. Remove meat with a slotted spoon to a warm serving dish. Bring cooking liquid to boiling and cook, stirring, until reduced and thickened. Taste and add salt, if needed. Pour over beef shanks. Sprinkle with parsley.

Makes 4 servings.

Sauerbraten-Style Steak Strips

Simmer strips of bottom round slowly with spices in a sweet-sour sauce for a German-inspired main dish to serve with noodles and—contrary to the rule of thumb that red wines taste best with beef—a chilled Rhine or Mosel.

1 pound bottom round, fat trimmed
Salt, pepper and flour
1 tablespoon *each* salad oil and butter or margarine
¼ cup red wine vinegar
1 cup dry white wine (such as Rhine or Chablis)
1 medium onion, thinly sliced and separated into rings
½ bay leaf
¼ teaspoon cinnamon
Dash *each* ground allspice and cloves
2 tablespoons raisins
1 gingersnap, finely crushed

1. Cut meat across the grain into ¼-inch-thick strips about 2 inches long and 1 inch wide. Sprinkle lightly with salt and pepper, then dust with flour, shaking off excess. Brown, about half at a time, in mixture of heated oil and butter in a large deep frying pan.

2. Return all the browned meat to the pan. Mix in vinegar, wine, onion, bay leaf, spices and raisins. Bring to boiling, cover tightly, reduce heat and simmer until meat is very tender, about 2 hours. Remove bay leaf. Salt to taste. Stir in gingersnap crumbs.

Makes 4 servings.

Beef brisket and vegetables makes an elegant all-in-one pot dinner.

Sauté top round with eggplant, herbs.

Beef and Eggplant Sauté

A good buffet dish, you can make this stew ahead and reheat it, to serve with noodles, green salad and red wine.

1 small eggplant (1 to 1½ lbs.)
Salt
½ cup olive oil or salad oil
(approximately)
2 to 3 pounds cubed boneless top
round, with fat trimmed
1 large onion, finely chopped
2 cloves garlic, minced or pressed
2 large tomatoes, peeled and
chopped
1 tablespoon tomato paste
½ teaspoon *each* salt and crum-
bled basil and rosemary
⅛ teaspoon *each* nutmeg and
white pepper
¼ cup dry red wine
Chopped parsley, for garnish

1. Remove stem and cut unpeeled eggplant into ¾-inch cubes. Spread on several thicknesses of paper towels; sprinkle with salt. Let eggplant stand for 20 minutes. Use paper towels to blot surface moisture.

2. Heat ¼ cup of the oil in a large frying pan. Brown eggplant cubes in heated oil, removing and reserving browned eggplant and adding more oil, 1 tablespoon at a time, as needed.

3. When all the eggplant is browned, brown beef cubes well on all sides in the same frying pan. Mix in onion and garlic; cook and stir until onion is soft.

4. Add tomatoes, tomato paste, salt, basil, rosemary, nutmeg, pepper and wine. Bring to boiling, cover, reduce heat and simmer for 2 to 2½ hours, until meat is very tender.

5. Gently stir in browned eggplant, cover again and continue cooking for 10 to 15 minutes longer, until eggplant is tender. Salt to taste. Sprinkle with chopped parsley.

Makes 6 to 8 servings.

Caraway Beef Paprika

Caraway seeds give this thick stew a middle European flavor complemented by broad noodles, rye bread and dark beer. The dish uses the center section of a chuck roast that you may have separated from the two more tender parts.

2 to 2½ pounds center section beef
chuck (from under blade bone,
see page 7), with fat trimmed
2 tablespoons butter or margarine
1 tablespoon salad oil
½ pound mushrooms, sliced
3 medium onions, finely chopped
1 clove garlic, minced or pressed
1 can (6 oz.) tomato paste
1 cup dry white wine
1 tablespoon paprika
1 bay leaf
1 teaspoon salt
½ teaspoon caraway seeds
⅛ teaspoon pepper
½ cup sour cream

1. Cut beef into bite-size cubes. Brown, about half at a time, in heated mixture of butter and oil in a large frying pan or Dutch oven, removing meat as it browns. When all the meat is browned, brown mushrooms lightly; remove from pan. In the same pan cook onions, stirring occasionally, until they brown lightly.

2. Return beef and mushrooms and their juices to pan. Mix in garlic, tomato paste, wine and seasonings. Bring to boiling, cover, reduce heat and simmer for about 2½ hours or until beef is very tender.

3. Just before serving, mix in sour cream, stirring over low heat until hot but not boiling. Salt to taste.

Makes 6 servings.

Provençale Beef Rolls

A ground ham filling gives these tender beef rolls a smoky flavor. The generous red sauce is good with fluffy rice.

2 pounds boneless top round,
about ½ inch thick
Ham Filling (recipe follows)
Flour
2 tablespoons olive oil or salad oil
1 medium onion, finely chopped
2 cloves garlic, minced or pressed
¼ pound mushrooms, quartered
½ cup *each* tomato juice and
dry red wine
Salt (optional)
Chopped parsley, for garnish

1. Cut meat into 6 to 8 pieces of equal size, trimming off any fat. Place each piece between sheets of waxed paper and pound, using the flat side of a mallet, until meat is less than ¼ inch thick. Spread each piece with Ham Filling, then tuck in sides and roll up firmly. Fasten ends with small metal skewers, or tie firmly at each end with clean white string.

2. Coat meat rolls lightly with flour, shaking off excess. Brown well on all sides in heated oil in a large frying pan. Add onion, garlic and mushrooms, stirring to brown lightly. Pour on tomato juice and wine, bring to boiling, reduce heat, cover and simmer for about 2½ hours, until meat is very tender when tested with a fork.

3. Remove beef rolls to a warm serving dish. Skim fat from pan liquid, then bring it to boiling and cook, stirring to loosen brown bits from pan, until sauce is reduced and slightly thickened. Taste and add salt, if needed. Pour sauce over beef rolls. Sprinkle with parsley and serve.

Makes 6 to 8 servings.

Ham Filling: Trim fat from and grind smoked pork shoulder picnic, using fine blade of food chopper, to make 1 cup. Sauté 1 small onion (finely chopped) in 1 tablespoon olive oil or salad oil until beginning to brown; remove from heat and stir in 1 clove garlic (minced or pressed), ground ham and ½ teaspoon crumbled Italian herb seasoning or *herbes de Provence*.

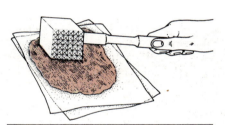

Use side of mallet to flatten meat.

Spread each piece of meat with Ham Filling.

Fold in sides, then roll up rectangles of pounded meat to enclose filling snugly; fasten with skewers or string.

Short ribs cook with such Mexican seasonings as cumin and cilantro.

Mexican Short Ribs

Flavored with oranges and green olives and spiced with cumin, this meaty dish is good with rice and hot buttered corn tortillas.

**4 pounds beef short ribs, cut in serving pieces
  Salt, pepper and flour
2 tablespoons olive oil or salad oil
1 large onion, thinly sliced and separated into rings
1 clove garlic, minced or pressed
1 can (1 lb.) tomatoes
1 cup dry red wine
1 teaspoon grated orange rind
  Juice of 1 orange
½ cup sliced pimiento-stuffed green olives
⅛ teaspoon cayenne
1 teaspoon ground cumin
  Chopped cilantro (fresh coriander, also known as Chinese parsley) or parsley, for garnish**

1. Sprinkle short ribs with salt and pepper, then coat lightly with flour, shaking off excess. Brown short ribs, about half at a time, in heated oil in a large frying pan or Dutch oven, removing them from pan as they brown. When all the ribs have been browned, pour off most of the drippings. In fat remaining in pan, cook onion rings and garlic until onion is tender and lightly browned.

2. Return browned short ribs to pan with tomatoes (coarsely chopped) and their liquid, wine, orange rind, orange juice, olives, cayenne and cumin. Bring to boiling, reduce heat, cover and simmer until meat is very tender, 2½ to 3 hours.

3. Remove short ribs to a warm serving dish and keep warm. Bring sauce to boiling, stirring occasionally, and boil, uncovered, until reduced and slightly thickened. Taste and add salt, if needed. Spoon sauce over meat. Sprinkle short ribs with chopped cilantro or parsley.

Makes 6 servings.

Braised Eye of Round Steaks

The villainous eye of round—so lovely to look at, yet such a disappointment in tenderness—responds well to long, slow cooking, and tastes very good with curly egg noodles. When you buy an economical full-cut round steak (see page 7) and separate the top and bottom round for other uses, re-serve the compact eyes of round in the freezer until you have six to use in this savory dish. Accompany it with steamed broccoli spears.

**6 eye of round steaks (about 2½ lbs.)
  Salt, seasoned pepper and flour
1 tablespoon *each* butter or margarine and salad oil
3 medium onions, thinly sliced
1 clove garlic, minced or pressed
¾ teaspoon dry mustard
1 teaspoon Italian herb seasoning or *herbes de Provence*
1 small can (12 oz.) vegetable juice cocktail**

1. Sprinkle steaks with salt and seasoned pepper; coat lightly with flour. Heat butter and oil in a large, heavy frying pan; brown pieces of floured meat well on both sides.

2. Top with onions. Sprinkle with garlic, dry mustard and herb mixture. Pour on vegetable juice. Bring to boiling, cover, reduce heat and simmer for about 2½ hours, until meat is very tender. Salt to taste.

3. Serve the meat with the sauce spooned over.

Makes 6 servings.

Mexican Pork with Green Chiles

Here is a wonderful filling for burritos. Let each diner scoop the steaming meat filling into warm flour tortillas, then roll them up with toasted pine nuts or almonds, cilantro (fresh coriander, also known as Chinese parsley and available in Oriental markets) and steamed rice.

To warm flour tortillas, first use your fingertips to sprinkle lightly with water; then heat individually on a seasoned griddle. Tortillas should be steamy and pliable. Stack them as they are heated, cover, and keep warm in a low oven.

3 pounds lean boneless pork butt, cut in 1-inch cubes
2 tablespoons lard or shortening
2 large onions, chopped
2 cloves garlic, minced or pressed
1 large tomato, peeled and coarsely chopped
1 large can (7 oz.) diced green chiles
2 teaspoons salt
1 teaspoon ground cumin
¾ teaspoon crumbled oregano
¼ cup chopped fresh cilantro or 1 tablespoon dried cilantro
1 cup water
2 teaspoons lime or lemon juice
Toasted pine nuts or slivered almonds (directions follow)
Chopped fresh cilantro or parsley, for garnish
Warm flour tortillas
Rice

1. Brown meat, about a third at a time, in heated lard in a 5 to 6-quart Dutch oven. When all the meat is browned, pour off excess fat, if necessary.

2. Return meat and its juices to pan; add onions, garlic, tomato, green chiles, salt, cumin, oregano, cilantro and water. Bring to boiling, cover, reduce heat and simmer for about 2 hours, until meat is very tender.

3. Uncover and continue cooking at a gentle boil for about 20 minutes, stirring occasionally, until slightly thickened. Stir in lime or lemon juice. Taste and add salt, if needed.

4. To serve, sprinkle with pine nuts or almonds and chopped cilantro. Serve spooned into warm flour tortillas with a little rice (or, if you wish, spoon over rice in shallow bowls, and accompany with hot, buttered flour tortillas).

Makes 6 to 8 servings.

To toast pine nuts or almonds:
Spread ½ to 1 cup pine nuts or slivered almonds in a shallow pan. Bake in a 350° oven for 8 to 10 minutes, stirring once or twice, until lightly browned.

Joyce's New Orleans Red Beans and Rice

From a city noted for its culinary excellence and diversity, here is a beloved family dish. It is said to have been a favorite meal for washday; one could start the beans cooking, then go about the numerous and exhausting tasks of heating water, feeding clothes through a hand-operated wringer and hanging them out to dry. By the time the laundry dried, the beans were ready for dinner. Even now, when automatic equipment does the wash, the dish tastes delicious.

1 pound dried red beans, rinsed and drained
2 quarts water
2 large onions, chopped
1 bay leaf
¼ teaspoon pepper
1 meaty ham bone, or 2 smoked ham hocks (1½ to 2 lbs.)
1 green pepper, finely chopped
1 tablespoon white vinegar
½ teaspoon Tabasco sauce
Salt (optional)
Fluffy rice

1. Bring beans and water to boiling in a 4 to 6-quart kettle or Dutch oven. Boil briskly for 2 minutes, then remove from heat, cover and let beans stand for 1 hour.

2. Add onions, bay leaf, pepper and ham bone or ham hocks. Bring to boiling, cover, reduce heat and simmer for 3 hours. Remove ham bone or ham hocks. When cool enough to handle, remove and discard bones, fat and skin. Return meat to beans in chunks.

3. Mix in green pepper, vinegar and Tabasco sauce. Continue simmering, uncovered, for 2 to 2½ hours longer, stirring occasionally, until beans are thick and very tender. Salt to taste. Serve over rice.

Makes 6 servings.

Red Beans and Rice begins with ham bone.

Kentucky Burgoo

This traditional Southern stew was once a hunter's creation, rich with such small game as squirrel and rabbit. Now it is more likely to be made with a plump chicken and bony cuts of beef, pork, veal and lamb. It is so hearty that few side dishes are needed—perhaps just a leafy salad and a good bread. Burgoo is traditional at Louisville parties during the week before the Kentucky Derby.

Burgoo takes a long time to cook—a total of 7 to 9 hours. If you wish, you can begin it one day and complete it the next. Cook the meats and chicken for several hours, remove the bones, return the meat to the broth, then refrigerate it overnight. The following day, skim the fat from the broth, reheat it and add the vegetables to cook 4 or 5 hours longer.

2 pounds *each* pork, veal, beef and lamb shanks
1 large chicken (about 4 lbs.), preferably a stewing hen
5 quarts water
6 *each* onions, medium potatoes and carrots
1 large can (28 oz.) tomato purée
2 green peppers, seeded and cut in strips
2 cups cabbage, shredded
1 package (10 oz.) frozen baby lima beans, thawed
1 cup chopped celery
2 small dried red chile peppers, crushed
2 tablespoons salt
2 ears corn
Worcestershire sauce
½ cup chopped parsley

1. Place meats and chicken in a very large pot (about 15 quarts), add water and bring to boiling. Reduce heat, cover and simmer for 3 to 4 hours until meats are so tender they fall from the bones.

2. Remove meat and chicken from the broth; cool slightly. Separate meat from the bones, discarding bones and chicken skin. Return meat in large chunks to the cooking liquid.

3. Chop onions; cut potatoes in ½-inch cubes; slice carrots thinly. Add prepared vegetables, along with tomato purée, green peppers, cabbage, lima beans, celery, dried red peppers and salt to the meat and broth. Simmer, uncovered, until thickened, about 4 to 5 hours longer. Stir frequently as the mixture becomes thick.

4. About 15 minutes before serving, cut kernels of corn from the cobs and add corn to the burgoo. Season to taste with salt and Worcestershire sauce. Stir in parsley. Serve in broad soup bowls.

Makes 12 to 15 servings.

Chicken Arlesienne

Just a pinch of saffron imparts a very special flavor to this chicken dish from the South of France. Accompany with rice, zucchini cooked just until tender-crisp, and bread sticks.

3 to 3½-pound frying chicken, quartered
Salt and white pepper
2 tablespoons butter or margarine
1 small onion, finely chopped
1 clove garlic, minced or pressed
¼ teaspoon *each* crumbled thyme and rosemary
Pinch saffron threads or powdered saffron
1 teaspoon Dijon mustard
1 small jar (2 oz.) sliced pimiento
1 can (8 oz.) tomato sauce
⅓ cup dry white wine
½ cup thawed frozen peas

1. Sprinkle chicken pieces with salt and white pepper. Brown lightly on both sides in heated butter in a large deep frying pan. Sprinkle with onion, garlic, thyme, rosemary and saffron. Mix mustard, pimiento (and its juice), tomato sauce and wine; pour sauce mixture over chicken.

2. Bring to boiling, cover, reduce heat and simmer until chicken is tender, about 50 minutes. Remove chicken pieces to a heated serving dish and keep warm.

3. Skim and discard fat from cooking liquid, then bring it to boiling and cook, stirring, until slightly reduced and thickened. Mix in peas and cook, uncovered, for about 3 minutes longer, until they are heated through. Taste and add salt, if needed. Pour sauce over chicken and serve.

Makes 4 servings.

Chicken, Hunter's Style

A savory mixture of herbs, mushrooms, red wine and a touch of tomato gives chicken legs a clear brown sauce similar to that used for game. Accompany with baked new potatoes in their jackets.

6 chicken legs with thighs attached
Salt, pepper and paprika
2 tablespoons butter or margarine
1 tablespoon salad oil
3 shallots, finely chopped, *or* 3 tablespoons freeze-dried shallots
1 small tomato, peeled and chopped
¼ pound mushrooms, quartered
2 cloves garlic, minced or pressed
½ teaspoon dry mustard
¼ teaspoon *each* crumbled thyme and rosemary
2 tablespoons Beef Concentrate (see page 10), *or* 1 tablespoon powdered beef stock base
¾ cup dry red wine

1. Sprinkle chicken legs with salt, pepper and paprika. In a large heavy frying pan, heat together butter and oil until foamy. In butter mixture brown chicken legs slowly on all sides. Spoon off excess fat.

2. Sprinkle chicken with shallots, tomato, mushrooms, garlic, mustard, thyme and rosemary. Add Beef Concentrate and wine. Bring to boiling. Reduce heat, cover and simmer for about 1 hour, until chicken is tender.

3. Using a slotted spoon, remove chicken and mushrooms to a warm serving dish. Bring cooking liquid to boiling and cook, stirring, until reduced and thickened. Taste and add salt, if needed; pour the thickened sauce over chicken.

Makes 6 servings.

Sautéed Lamb with Spring Vegetables

Peas and asparagus added just at the end give this elegant stew a spring-time freshness. Accompany with small, buttered new potatoes cooked in their jackets; follow the main dish with a leafy green salad.

3¾ to 4½-pound lamb shoulder roast
Salt and white pepper
2 tablespoons butter or margarine
1 medium onion, finely chopped
1 small clove garlic, minced or pressed
¼ teaspoon *each* crumbled tarragon and rosemary
⅛ teaspoon *each* ground nutmeg and cloves
3 medium carrots, cut lengthwise in quarters
2 small turnips, quartered
1 cup dry white wine
½ cup fresh or thawed frozen peas
1 cup cut fresh asparagus (about 1-inch pieces)
1 teaspoon lemon juice
Chopped parsley, for garnish

1. Bone roast (see page 20), trim fat and cut meat into bite-size cubes (you should have about 4 cups).

2. Sprinkle meat with salt and white pepper. Brown, about half at a time, in heated butter in a large deep frying pan or Dutch oven. When all the lamb is browned, pour off fat and return lamb and its juices to pan.

3. Add onion, garlic, herbs, spices, carrots, turnips and wine. Bring to boiling, cover, reduce heat and simmer for 1½ to 2 hours, until meat is fork tender.

4. Uncover and mix in peas and asparagus. Continue cooking, uncovered, for 5 to 8 minutes longer, until green vegetables are tender-crisp. Using a slotted spoon, remove the lamb and

vegetables to a warm serving dish and keep warm.

5. Bring cooking liquid to boiling and cook, stirring, until reduced and slightly thickened. Mix in lemon juice. Taste and add salt, if needed. Pour sauce over the lamb and vegetables. Sprinkle with parsley and serve.

Makes 6 servings.

Fruited Lamb Curry

A versatile lamb shoulder provides the meat for this elegant curry. Accompany it with rice and a choice of condiments to sprinkle over each serving.

4 to 5-pound lamb shoulder roast
2 tablespoons butter or margarine
4 medium onions, thinly sliced and separated into rings
3 large tart green apples, peeled, cored and sliced
2 cloves garlic, minced or pressed
2 tablespoons *each* flour and curry powder
¼ cup golden raisins
1½ teaspoons ground ginger
1 stick cinnamon, broken in 2 pieces
1 teaspoon salt
1 cup *each* regular-strength beef broth (homemade or canned) and dry red wine
1 teaspoon lemon juice
Rice
Condiments: chopped dry-roast peanuts, toasted unsweetened coconut, chutney, sliced green onions, diced unpeeled cucumber, plain yogurt

1. Bone roast (see page 20), trim fat and cut into bite-size cubes (you should have at least 4 cups cubed meat).

2. Brown cubed lamb, about half at a time, in heated butter in a large frying pan or Dutch oven; remove meat as it browns. When all the meat is browned, pour off all but 2 tablespoons of the drippings. In fat remaining in pan, sauté onions until golden. Add apples and cook, stirring lightly, about 3 minutes longer. Mix in garlic, flour and curry powder.

3. Return meat and its juices to pan with raisins, ginger, cinnamon stick, salt, broth, wine and lemon juice. Bring to boiling, cover, reduce heat and simmer for 1½ to 2 hours, until meat is very tender and flavors are well blended.

4. Serve with rice; pass condiments in small bowls.

Makes 6 to 8 servings.

Lamb curry makes a festive dish. Condiments include (counterclockwise from top) peanuts, chutney, green onions, yogurt, coconut and chopped cucumber.

Accompany Veal Stew with Fresh Peas with butter-browned new potatoes.

Stew is special when made with fresh peas.

Veal Stew with Fresh Peas

Here is another delicate spring or summer stew, also made with veal. The tender veal chunks and bright green peas go well with butter-browned new potatoes. To complete the menu add a leafy green salad with your favorite dressing, French bread and butter, milk and a dry white wine. For dessert, indulge in some of spring's first strawberries.

> **2 pounds cubed boneless veal shoulder**
> **Salt, white pepper and paprika**
> **2 tablespoons butter or margarine**
> **1 tablespoon salad oil**
> **1 small onion, finely chopped**
> **1 medium tomato, peeled and chopped**
> **1 large carrot, cut in ¼-inch slices**
> **⅛ teaspoon crumbled tarragon**
> **¾ cup dry white wine**
> **½ cup shelled fresh peas, *or* thawed frozen peas**
> **Chopped parsley, for garnish**

1. Sprinkle veal with salt, white pepper and paprika. Heat butter with oil in a large heavy frying pan or Dutch oven. In butter mixture brown veal lightly on all sides. Add onion, tomato, carrot, tarragon and wine. Bring to boiling, cover, reduce heat and simmer for about 1½ hours, until veal is very tender.

2. Mix in peas and cook for 5 to 8 minutes longer, uncovered, until they are just tender. Salt to taste. Sprinkle with parsley and serve.

Makes 6 servings.

Veal Breast Braised with Tarragon

For this creamy stew, ask your meat dealer to cut through the veal breast bone in several places so you can separate the meat into 1-rib sections. Accompany the stew with noodles or rice and green or yellow wax beans.

> **3 to 3½-pound breast of veal, cut in serving pieces**
> **Salt, white pepper and nutmeg**
> **2 tablespoons butter**
> **1 tablespoon salad oil**
> **1½ teaspoons crumbled tarragon**
> **1 small onion, finely chopped**
> **¼ cup shredded carrot**
> **½ cup *each* dry white wine and whipping cream**
> **¼ cup chopped parsley**

1. Sprinkle pieces of veal generously with salt, pepper and nutmeg. In a large, heavy frying pan or Dutch oven, heat together butter and oil until foamy. In butter mixture brown veal lightly on all sides.

2. Sprinkle with tarragon, onion and carrot. Pour on wine. Bring to boiling, cover, reduce heat and simmer for about 2 hours, until veal is very tender. Remove veal to a serving dish and keep warm.

3. To pan juices add cream and 3 tablespoons of the parsley; bring to boiling. Cook, stirring, until reduced and thickened (large, shiny bubbles will form). Pour sauce over veal. Sprinkle with remaining 1 tablespoon parsley and serve.

Makes 4 servings.

Oven Stews

Using your oven to cook a stew enables you to prepare accompaniments using the same heat source—potatoes or other vegetables, a baked dessert, a bread to warm. Covered ceramic or enameled metal casseroles are ideal for oven stews; many are handsome enough to bring directly from oven to dinner table.

Oven Beef Stew

This easy oven stew is ideal for a busy day—you can simmer it in the oven for hours with no attention whatsoever. It is a big recipe and is ideal for a company buffet with a mixed green salad, noodles, green beans or broccoli and, for dessert, your favorite apple pastry.

4 pounds boneless beef chuck, cut in 1½-inch cubes
1 cup dry red wine
2 tablespoons brandy (optional)
⅓ cup chopped parsley
2 cloves garlic, mashed
¼ teaspoon *each* thyme and crumbled rosemary
1 bay leaf
2 medium onions, thinly sliced
½ cup flour
1 teaspoon *each* salt and paprika
¼ teaspoon pepper
6 carrots, cut in ½-inch slices
½ pound small whole mushrooms

1. Trim off any fat from meat cubes; place meat in large bowl. Add wine, brandy, parsley, garlic, herbs and onions; mix lightly. Cover and refrigerate 8 to 24 hours; remove meat, saving marinade.

2. Pat meat dry with paper towel. Mix flour, salt, paprika and pepper; coat cubed meat with flour mixture. Place about a third of the meat in a deep 4½ to 5-quart casserole. Top with half the carrots and mushrooms, another third of the meat, remaining vegetables and the last of the meat. Bring reserved marinade and onions to boiling; pour over meat.

3. Cover and bake in a 325° oven for about 4 hours, until meat is very tender. Discard bay leaf. Salt stew to taste. Garnish with chopped parsley.

Makes 8 to 10 servings.

Round Steak and Kidney Beans

Cubed bottom round with red kidney beans makes a hearty casserole that's great to take to a potluck supper or a tailgate picnic.

1 pound red kidney beans, rinsed and drained
6 cups water
½ pound pork link sausages
1 pound bottom round steak, fat trimmed and meat cut in about ¾-inch cubes
1 large onion, finely chopped
1 clove garlic, minced or pressed
1 teaspoon salt
½ teaspoon crushed rosemary
1 can (8 oz.) tomato sauce

1. In a large kettle bring to boiling the kidney beans and water. Boil vigorously 2 minutes. Cover, remove from heat and let stand 1 hour.

2. In a large deep frying pan or Dutch oven, brown the pork sausages well on all sides; remove from pan and reserve sausages as they brown. Pour off all but 2 tablespoons of the drippings. In sausage drippings brown round steak cubes very well on all sides. Add prepared beans and their liquid, onion, garlic, salt, rosemary and tomato sauce. Bring to boiling, stirring occasionally.

3. Transfer meat and bean mixture to a deep 3 to 4-quart casserole. Arrange sausages on top. Cover and bake in a 350° oven for about 3 hours, until beans and meat are tender.

Makes 6 servings.

Spicy Alsatian Meat and Vegetable Stew

In Alsace, the charming wine-growing region of eastern France, it is traditional to serve this stew at large family gatherings. Made with four different kinds of meat in an enormous casserole, it is taken out to be cooked in a baker's oven. But you can make it on a smaller scale in your own kitchen and it will still serve 8 to 10 dinner guests bountifully.

1 pound veal shanks, sliced 1 inch thick
2 pounds cubed boneless beef chuck
1 lamb shank (about 1 lb.)
1 pound boneless pork butt, cubed
1 cup dry white wine
2 large onions, thinly sliced
1 bay leaf
1 teaspoon whole white or black peppers
½ teaspoon *each* ground cinnamon and whole cloves
¼ teaspoon ground nutmeg
4 carrots, thinly sliced
2 leeks, thinly sliced (use part of tops)
4 medium boiling potatoes, thinly sliced

1. Place meats in a deep bowl; add wine, onions, bay leaf and spices. Mix lightly. Cover and marinate in refrigerator 8 hours or overnight.

2. Mix carrots and leeks and place in bottom of a deep 5-quart casserole. Then make layers of marinated meats, onions and potatoes until all are used, ending with a layer of potatoes on top. Pour on marinade.

3. Cover tightly and bake in a 450° oven 30 minutes; reduce heat to 350° and continue baking 3 hours, until meats are very tender. Salt to taste.

Makes 8 to 10 servings.

Layers of beef, mushrooms, herbs and onion make an easy oven stew.

Moroccan lamb shanks bake with honey, exotic spices and lemon.

Lamb Shanks with Honey and Spices

Inspired by the exotically flavored stews of Morocco, these lamb shanks are good accompanied by brown rice and a lettuce and tomato salad with a piquant oil-and-vinegar dressing.

    2 medium onions, thinly sliced
    1 tablespoon *each* butter or
      margarine and olive oil or salad
      oil
    1 clove garlic, minced or pressed
    1 teaspoon salt
    ½ teaspoon *each* ground turmeric
      and ginger
    ¼ teaspoon *each* ground allspice
      and coriander
    ¾ cup water
    ¼ cup honey
    2 cinnamon sticks
    4 to 5 pounds lamb shanks,
      cracked
    1 lemon, thinly sliced
      Brown rice

1. Sauté onions in mixture of butter and oil in a large frying pan until limp but not browned. Mix in garlic, salt and ground spices to coat onions; simmer about 2 minutes. Mix in water, honey and cinnamon sticks; bring to boiling, then remove from heat.

2. Arrange lamb shanks in a deep casserole just large enough to hold them in a single layer. Pour on onion mixture. Arrange lemon slices over lamb. Cover and bake in a 350° oven for about 2 hours, until lamb is very tender.

3. Remove lamb and lemons to a serving dish and keep warm. Skim fat from cooking liquid; boil it to reduce and thicken it slightly. Pour over lamb and serve with brown rice.

Makes 4 to 6 servings.

Savory Oven Pork Stew

Both this stew and the beef stew on page 71 are made in the manner of a French *daube*—the meat is seasoned and floured, then layered with vegetables and cooked in wine in a deep ceramic casserole. This one requires no marinating before baking, so it is fairly quick to assemble. An easy accompaniment is baked potatoes. Place in the oven during the last hour the stew is cooking.

    5 pounds country-style spareribs,
      cut in serving pieces
      Salt, pepper, paprika and flour
    1 medium onion, thinly sliced and
      separated into rings
    ½ pound small white boiling onions
    ½ cup slivered smoked pork
      shoulder picnic, or ham
    2 cloves garlic, minced or pressed
    1 carrot, shredded
    ¼ pound mushrooms, quartered
    1 cup dry red wine
    2 tablespoons Beef Concentrate
      (see page 10), *or* 1 tablespoon
      powdered beef stock base
    ½ teaspoon *each* crumbled
      marjoram and rosemary
    ⅛ teaspoon ground allspice
    1 bay leaf
    2 tablespoons brandy (optional)
      Chopped parsley, for garnish

1. Sprinkle spareribs with salt, pepper and paprika; coat with flour. Mix sliced and boiling onions, ham strips, garlic, carrot and mushrooms. Place about a third of the spareribs in a deep 5-quart casserole; cover with half of the vegetable mixture. Repeat with another layer of spareribs and remaining vegetables. Top with remaining spareribs.

2. Heat together wine, Beef Concentrate, marjoram, rosemary, allspice and bay leaf, stirring until the concentrate dissolves. Add brandy (if used); pour mixture over spareribs.

3. Cover and bake in a 350° oven for about 3 hours, until meat is very tender. Using a slotted spoon, remove meat and onions to a warm serving dish; keep warm. Skim and discard fat from cooking liquid. Pour liquid into a saucepan and boil until reduced and slightly thickened; salt to taste. Pour over meat. Sprinkle with parsley.

Makes 8 servings.

Country-Style Spareribs in Ratatouille

Ratatouille (say rah-tah-TOO-ye), that splendid melange of garlic seasoned vegetables, colorfully sets off oven-roasted spareribs.

    1 large eggplant (about 1½ lbs.)
      Salt
    ½ cup olive oil or salad oil
      (approximately)
    3 cloves garlic, minced or pressed
    1 large onion, chopped
    1 *each* red and green bell pepper,
      seeded and cut in strips
    ½ teaspoon *each* salt and crumbled
      basil
    ¼ teaspoon *each* crumbled thyme
      and rosemary
    ¼ cup chopped parsley
    2 large tomatoes, peeled and
      coarsely chopped
    4 to 5 pounds country-style
      spareribs, cut in serving pieces

1. Cut unpeeled eggplant into ¾-inch cubes. Spread in a single layer on several thicknesses of paper towels. Sprinkle liberally with salt; let stand 20 minutes. Then blot up surface moisture with paper towels. Heat about half of the oil with garlic in a large frying pan over moderately high heat. Add eggplant and brown lightly on all sides, stirring often and adding more oil as needed. As eggplant browns, remove it from pan and transfer it to a large broad casserole (at least 4-quart size). To the oil remaining in the pan, add onion and cook until soft and lightly browned.

2. Mix cooked onions, red and green pepper, seasonings, parsley, tomatoes and browned eggplant in casserole. Cover and bake in a 350° oven 1 hour.

3. Meanwhile, arrange spareribs in a single layer in an open roasting pan; sprinkle with salt. Place in same oven with vegetable casserole. At the end of 1 hour, arrange spareribs over vegetables, cover and continue baking 45 minutes. Uncover; bake about 15 minutes until ribs are tender and well browned. Remove spareribs to a platter. Skim fat from ratatouille; spoon ratatouille over spareribs.

Makes 6 servings.

Rich Red Spareribs

Here is a delicious and easy way to bake spareribs in a covered casserole. Corn-on-the-cob completes the meal.

4 pounds meaty spareribs, cut in serving pieces
Water
¼ cup *each* soy sauce, lemon juice and honey
½ cup catsup
½ teaspoon ground ginger
1 clove garlic, minced or pressed

1. Place spareribs in a large frying pan, Dutch oven or electric skillet. Add water to cover. Bring to boiling, cover, reduce heat and simmer 30 minutes. Drain well, patting spareribs dry with paper towels.

2. Arrange spareribs in a broad 2 to 3-quart casserole. Mix soy sauce, lemon juice, honey, catsup, ginger and garlic until smooth. Pour over spareribs, coating them well with sauce. Cover and bake in a 350° oven for 1 to 1½ hours, basting two or three times with sauce, until spareribs are tender and well browned.

Makes 4 to 6 servings.

Yankee Clipper Chicken

A straightforward dish with unadorned natural flavors, this vegetable-baked chicken goes well with rice or mashed potatoes and hot biscuits with honey.

3 to 3½-pound frying chicken, cut in quarters (see page 9)
Salt, white pepper, nutmeg and flour
1 tablespoon *each* butter or margarine and salad oil
4 carrots, sliced about ⅜-inch thick
1 onion, thinly sliced
½ cup chopped celery
¼ cup *each* regular-strength chicken broth (homemade or canned) and dry vermouth

1. Sprinkle quartered chicken lightly on all sides with salt, pepper and nutmeg; then coat with flour, shaking off excess. In a large frying pan heat together butter and oil; brown chicken well on all sides and place in a single layer, skin-side up, in a 10-inch square casserole.

2. Pour off most of the drippings in the frying pan and sauté carrots, onion and celery until onion is tender and beginning to brown. Add chicken broth and vermouth, stirring to loosen pan drippings. Pour vegetable mixture over chicken.

3. Cover and bake in a 325° oven for 1 hour, until chicken and vegetables are tender. Uncover and bake 10 to 15 minutes. Serve with vegetables and sauce spooned over chicken.

Makes 4 servings.

Country Captain

This favorite Southern dish with chicken probably had its origins in India. However it made its way to our shores, it is a good choice for a party buffet, served with green beans.

2 frying chickens, about 3 pounds *each*
Salt and pepper
2 to 3 tablespoons butter or margarine
1 large onion, finely chopped
1½ cups long grain rice
2 green peppers, seeded and chopped
1 large clove garlic, minced or pressed
½ cup raisins
2 teaspoons curry powder
1 can (1 lb.) tomatoes
1¼ cups regular-strength chicken broth (homemade or canned)
¾ teaspoon crumbled thyme
½ cup slivered blanched almonds

1. Cut chickens into serving pieces (see page 9), reserving back bones, breast bones, necks and giblets for broth or other uses. Sprinkle lightly with salt and pepper. In a large frying pan, brown chicken pieces on all sides in heated butter, 4 or 5 at a time (do not crowd), removing them from pan as they brown.

2. When all the chicken is browned, stir onion and rice in the same pan until onion is soft and lightly browned. Mix in green peppers, garlic, raisins and curry powder; cook and stir for about 3 minutes. Add tomatoes (coarsely chopped) and their liquid, broth and thyme, stirring to mix in brown bits from pan. Transfer the rice mixture to a broad 4-quart casserole. Arrange chicken pieces over the rice, in a single layer if possible, pouring on any accumulated juices.

3. Cover and bake in a 375° oven for 45 minutes, until chicken is tender. Remove chicken and stir rice well; replace chicken on rice. Sprinkle chicken with almonds and continue baking, uncovered, about 15 minutes longer, until chicken and almonds are golden.

Makes 8 servings.

Spicy curried Country Captain is delicious for a company buffet.

Singapore Chicken

Colorful with pineapple, mandarin oranges and sliced apples, this baked chicken is attractive served on a bed of white rice.

2 small whole chickens, about 2½ pounds *each*
½ teaspoon ground ginger
1 tablespoon curry powder
1 teaspoon salt
2 tablespoons butter or margarine
1 small can (8 oz.) sliced pineapple
1 can (11 oz.) mandarin oranges
1 tart apple (unpeeled), cored and sliced
⅓ cup whipping cream
1 tablespoon lemon juice
Sliced pimiento, for garnish

1. Cut chickens in quarters, reserving giblets for another use. Mix ginger, curry powder and salt. Sprinkle chicken with seasonings. Melt butter in a large shallow baking dish (about 13 by 9 inches) in a 350° oven. Arrange chicken quarters, skin side down, in melted butter. Bake, uncovered, for 30 minutes.

2. Meanwhile, drain pineapple and oranges. Halve pineapple slices. Turn chicken; cover with pineapple slices, mandarin oranges and apple slices. Pour on cream and lemon juice. Cover and continue baking about 40 minutes longer, until the chicken and apples are tender.

3. Uncover, baste with pan drippings and continue baking about 15 minutes longer, until chicken is well browned. Garnish with pimiento slices.

Makes 8 servings.

Gascon Beans and Chicken Gizzards

If you have saved and frozen the gizzards from chickens purchased whole, here is a delicious way to cook them: a sort of simplified *cassoulet*. Even such a lowly thing as a chicken gizzard becomes tender and flavorful when it bakes for several hours in a bean pot.

1 pound small white beans, rinsed and drained
6 cups water
6 slices bacon, cut in squares
1 pound chicken gizzards (15 to 20), cut in halves
3 medium onions, thinly sliced and separated into rings
2 cloves garlic, minced or pressed
1 bay leaf
1 teaspoon salt
½ teaspoon crumbled marjoram
⅛ teaspoon white pepper
1 pound Polish sausage
1 can (8 oz.) tomato sauce
Buttery Bread Crumbs (directions follow)

1. Place beans in a large bowl, add water and let stand overnight. (Or, if you prefer, bring beans and water to boiling in a 4-quart kettle, boil briskly for 2 minutes, then remove from heat and let stand, covered, 1 hour.)

2. In a large frying pan, brown bacon; drain on paper towels. Pour off all but 2 tablespoons of the bacon drippings. Brown chicken gizzards slowly in reserved drippings, removing them as they brown. In the same pan, cook sliced onions until limp and beginning to brown.

3. To soaked beans add bacon, gizzards, onions, garlic, bay leaf, salt, marjoram and pepper. Transfer to a deep 4-quart casserole, cover and bake in a 350° oven for about 3 hours, until beans are tender.

4. Cut sausage in 2-inch chunks, and pierce each piece in several places with a fork. To cooked beans add sausage and tomato sauce, mixing lightly. Top with bread crumbs. Return to oven and continue baking, uncovered, about 45 minutes longer, until crumbs are well browned.

Makes 6 to 8 servings.

Buttery Bread Crumbs: In a frying pan heat together 1 tablespoon salad oil and 2 tablespoons butter or margarine until foamy. Stir in ½ cup soft French bread crumbs until coated.

Clay Pot Stews

Dome-lidded terra cotta cookers designed for baking chicken and meats are an attractive kitchen accessory to be found in most cookware shops. If you have one you have used only for chicken, you may not be aware of its considerable versatility.

A new clay pot with an unglazed interior should be seasoned before the first use to dispel its earthy smell and to help temper and strengthen the pottery. Here is a good method: Rub the

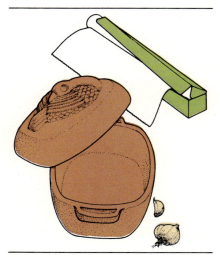

Line unglazed clay baker with parchment.

pot, inside and out (including the cover), with peeled garlic. A very large pot may require several cloves. Then place the pot in a 350° oven, fill it almost to the top with hot water, cover and bake for 4 to 6 hours. Pour out any remaining water, wipe dry with paper towels and the pot is ready.

Lining an *unglazed* pot with baking parchment will keep fats, oils and other food flavors from being absorbed by the porous pottery and mingling—perhaps unappetizingly—with subsequent foods cooked in it.

All of the following stews, although designed to be baked in clay cookers, can also be prepared as oven stews in any ceramic ovenware casserole of appropriate size and shape. If the interior is a smooth, shiny or glazed surface, it is unnecessary to use the parchment paper lining.

Chicken and Lentils in Clay

Chicken roasts to moist perfection surrounded by a savory mixture of lentils and vegetables in a clay cooker.

3 to 3½-pound frying chicken
1 cup lentils, rinsed and drained
1 large clove garlic, minced or pressed
1 medium onion, thinly sliced and separated into rings
¼ cup finely chopped celery
½ cup slivered smoked pork shoulder picnic, or ham
1 medium carrot, shredded
¼ cup chopped parsley
1 small bay leaf
½ teaspoon salt
⅛ teaspoon pepper
1 cup regular-strength beef broth (homemade or canned)
½ cup dry red wine
1 teaspoon dry mustard

1. Rinse chicken; pat dry. Coarsely chop liver and reserve. (Discard remaining giblets, or save them for another use.) Line a 3-quart unglazed clay cooker with parchment paper, trimming paper even with rim of baking dish. Place chicken, breast up, within parchment.

2. Place lentils around chicken. Combine garlic, onion, celery, ham, carrot, parsley and chicken liver; place mixture and bay leaf atop lentils. Sprinkle with salt and pepper. Heat together beef broth, wine and mustard; pour over chicken.

3. Cover and bake in a 375° oven, stirring lentils occasionally, until chicken is browned and lentils are tender, about 3 hours. Carve chicken and serve with lentils.

Makes 4 servings.

Cooked with lentils in a clay pot, a whole chicken is a generous meal for four.

Beef Baked in Beer

Oniony and delicious, this beef stew is a version of the notable Belgian dish, *carbonnades.* The beef cooks to estimable tenderness in beer, which gives a subtle, malty flavor. Accompany the stew with fluffy mashed potatoes and a green vegetable.

3 pounds bottom round, cut in
  1-inch cubes
  Salt, pepper and flour
5 large onions, thinly sliced
1 clove garlic, minced or pressed
1 small bay leaf
½ teaspoon crumbled rosemary
1 can (12 oz.) beer
2 tablespoons red wine vinegar
1 teaspoon Dijon-style mustard
  Chopped parsley, for garnish

1. Sprinkle cubed meat with salt and pepper, then coat lightly with flour. Mix onions, garlic, bay leaf and rosemary. Line a 4 to 5-quart unglazed clay cooker with parchment paper, trimming paper about 2 inches above rim of baking dish.

2. Alternate layers of the onion mixture and beef cubes in parchment-lined casserole, beginning and ending with onions. Pour on beer. Cover and bake in a 350° oven for 4 to 4½ hours, until meat is very tender.

3. Mix in vinegar and mustard. Taste and add salt, if needed. Sprinkle with parsley and serve.

Makes 6 to 8 servings.

Curried Oxtails in Clay

Although you may think of oxtails strictly in connection with soup, they can also make a delicious stew. Serve this colorful dish with rice.

⅓ cup flour
1 teaspoon salt
1 tablespoon *each* paprika and
  curry powder
4 to 4½ pounds meaty oxtails, cut
  in segments
1 large onion, chopped
½ pound mushrooms, sliced
1 red bell pepper, seeded and cut
  in thin strips
1 clove garlic, minced or pressed
¾ cup *each* dry sherry and
  regular-strength beef broth
  (homemade or canned)
  Cucumber slices, for garnish

1. Mix flour, salt, paprika and curry powder. Coat oxtails with flour mixture, reserving any that remains. Line a 2½ to 3-quart unglazed clay cooker with parchment paper, trimming paper about 2 inches above rim of dish. Place oxtails within paper.

2. Top with onion, mushrooms, red pepper and garlic. Pour on sherry and broth. Cover. Bake in a 350° oven,

stirring once or twice, for about 3½ hours, until oxtails are very tender.

3. With a slotted spoon, transfer meat and vegetables to a serving bowl and keep them warm. Skim fat from cooking liquid. Pour liquid into a saucepan. Smoothly mix 1 tablespoon of the reserved flour mixture with 2 tablespoons cold water; stir into liquid. Bring to boiling, stirring constantly, until thickened. Simmer 3 to 5 minutes. Pour sauce over meat. Garnish with cucumbers.

Makes 6 servings.

Italian Veal Shanks in Tomato Sauce

A big clay pot is ideal for veal shanks cooked in the Italian manner. The marrow of *osso buco* (literally, "hollow bones") is prized and should be scooped out and enjoyed. The traditional accompaniment for this dish is a saffron-spiced risotto, but it is also good with green noodles.

6 pounds meaty veal shanks, cut in
  2-inch lengths
  Salt, white pepper and flour
1 carrot, shredded
3 cloves garlic, minced or pressed
1 medium onion, finely chopped
1 can (1 lb.) tomatoes
½ cup dry red wine
1 tablespoon salt
1 teaspoon sugar
½ teaspoon crumbled rosemary
¼ teaspoon sage
⅓ cup finely chopped parsley
1 tablespoon grated lemon peel

1. Sprinkle veal shanks with salt and pepper; coat lightly with flour. Line a 3½ to 5-quart unglazed clay cooker with parchment paper, trimming paper about 2 inches above rim of dish. Place half of the veal shanks within the parchment.

2. Mix carrot, about two-thirds of the minced garlic (reserve a third for topping) and onion. Top veal shanks with vegetable mixture, then remaining veal shanks. Heat together tomatoes (coarsely chopped) and their liquid, wine, salt, sugar, rosemary and sage. Pour over veal shanks. Cover. Bake in a 350° oven for 2½ to 3 hours, until meat is very tender.

3. With a slotted spoon, remove veal shanks to a serving dish and keep them warm. Pour cooking liquid into a saucepan, bring it to boiling and cook, stirring, until reduced and thickened. Salt, if needed. Mix remaining garlic with parsley and lemon peel; stir about half of the mixture into cooking liquid and simmer for 2 minutes. Pour over veal shanks. Sprinkle with remaining parsley mixture.

Makes 6 servings.

Slow Cooker Stews

Electric slow cookers offer many possibilities for making stews. Because they cook so very gently and are tightly covered, little evaporation from the cooking food occurs, and meats and poultry remain moist and juicy. This also means that if you are adapting a favorite stew recipe to slow cooker use, you should cut back on the cooking liquid.

It is possible that cold food placed in a slow cooker could take so long to reach a safe cooking temperature that some food spoilage might occur. Therefore, the following slow cooker recipes begin with hot food and start it cooking at the pre-heated "high" cooking temperature.

Piedmontese Pot Roast

This moistly tender, Italian-style pot roast has a rich, dark wine sauce. Serve the meat with butter-browned potato chunks and steamed Swiss chard or fresh spinach with lemon wedges to squeeze over the vegetable for a tart flavor accent.

3½ to 4-pound boneless rump roast
1 teaspoon salt
¼ teaspoon pepper
½ teaspoon rosemary, crumbled
1 large onion, chopped
1 clove garlic, mashed
2 medium carrots, shredded
1 stalk celery, chopped
1 small bay leaf
10 whole cloves
1 cup dry red wine
1 tablespoon tomato paste
¼ cup rum or brandy

1. Rub the roast with a mixture of salt, pepper and rosemary. Brown roast, with fat side up, in an open roasting pan in a 500° oven for 15 minutes; discard the fat.

2. Mix onion, garlic, carrots, celery, bay leaf and cloves. Place about half of the vegetable mixture in electric slow cooker preheated on "high" setting. Top with browned roast. Surround with remaining vegetable mixture. Mix wine and tomato paste; pour over meat and vegetables.

3. Cover and cook at "high" for about 5 hours, until meat is very tender. Remove meat and keep it warm while preparing sauce. Discard bay leaf. Skim and discard fat from cooking liquid, then purée liquid and vegetables in blender until thick and smooth. Pour into a saucepan and reheat to serving temperature (boil several minutes to reduce, if sauce is too thin). Stir in rum or brandy and heat several minutes longer. Salt to taste. Serve the sauce over sliced beef.

Makes 6 to 8 servings.

Use an electric slow cooker for a hearty dish of lima beans and ham; serve with cole slaw and corn muffins.

Rosemary Round Steak

Layers of tomatoes, onions, beef and seasonings all blend their flavors appealingly during hours of slow cooking while the meat becomes tender.

**2 pounds top round, about ¾ inch thick, cut in serving-size pieces
  Salt, pepper and flour
2 tablespoons butter or margarine
1 tablespoon salad oil
½ teaspoon crumbled rosemary
¼ teaspoon garlic powder
2 teaspoons Dijon-style mustard
½ cup regular-strength beef broth (homemade or canned)
3 large tomatoes, peeled and thinly sliced
1 medium onion, sliced and separated into rings
  Chopped parsley, for garnish**

1. Trim fat from pieces of meat; sprinkle with salt and pepper, then coat with flour. Brown well on both sides in mixture of heated butter and oil in a large frying pan, removing pieces of meat as they brown to an electric slow cooker preheated to "high". Sprinkle with rosemary and garlic powder.

2. After removing all the meat, pour off and discard fat. Add mustard and broth to pan drippings, stirring until smooth and well blended, loosening brown bits from pan; set pan aside.

3. Over meat make layers of tomatoes, then onion rings. Pour on liquid mixture from frying pan. Cook at "high" setting 1 hour. Reduce heat to "low," and continue cooking until meat is very tender, 6 to 8 hours longer, stirring occasionally, if possible, during the last 2 hours. Salt to taste. Sprinkle with parsley.

Makes 6 servings.

Slow Cooker Corned Beef and Lentils

Cooked on top of the range, corned beef may remain tenaciously tough, but the slow cooker transforms it. Lentils absorb the good corned beef flavors deliciously.

**3 to 3½-pound corned beef brisket
  Water
1 package (12 or 14 oz., about 2 cups) lentils, rinsed and drained
1 stalk celery, finely chopped
1 carrot, shredded
½ pound small white boiling onions
¼ cup chopped parsley
1 tablespoon mixed pickling spice, tied in a square of cheesecloth
2 cups hot water
½ cup dry white wine
  Dijon-style mustard**

1. Rinse corned beef in cold running water to remove as much salt as possible, then place it in a 4 to 6-quart Dutch oven. Cover with 2 quarts cold water and bring it to boiling; drain and discard salty water. Add remaining ingredients, except mustard; and bring the mixture to boiling. Cover and boil gently for 15 minutes.

2. Transfer ingredients to an electric slow cooker preheated on "high" setting. Reduce heat to "low" and cook, covered, for about 8 hours, until corned beef is very tender.

3. Discard cheesecloth with seasonings. Arrange sliced corned beef on a warm deep platter. Remove lentils with a slotted spoon, place them around the meat and serve. Pass Dijon-style mustard.

Makes 6 to 8 servings.

Ham and Lima Bean Pot

This generous pot of well-seasoned dried lima beans is simmered with large cubes of economical smoked pork shoulder or leftover ham. It is fine for a picnic or other open-air family gathering. Crisp cole slaw and homemade corn muffins or corn sticks are favorite accompaniments.

**2 medium onions, sliced
1 green pepper, seeded and chopped
  Fat trimmed from ham
2 to 3 cups cubed cooked smoked pork shoulder picnic, or ham
1 pound dried baby lima beans, rinsed and drained
4½ cups water
¼ cup *each* catsup and dark molasses
1 tablespoon white vinegar
¼ teaspoon Tabasco sauce
1 teaspoon dry mustard
2 tablespoons butter or margarine**

1. In a 4 to 6-quart Dutch oven cook onions and green pepper in fat trimmed from ham until onions are limp and lightly browned. Mix in ham, beans, water, catsup, molasses, vinegar, Tabasco and dry mustard. Boil gently, uncovered, and stir occasionally, for 15 minutes.

2. Transfer mixture to an electric slow cooker preheated on "high" setting. Dot with butter. Cover and cook for 1 hour; reduce heat to "low" and continue cooking about 6 hours longer, until beans are tender, stirring occasionally, if possible, during the last 2 hours. Taste and add salt, if needed.

Makes 6 servings.

Make-Ahead Casseroles and Meat Pies

Advance planning makes both elegance and economy possible with these dishes and menu ideas for entertaining friends or family.

If there is anything that makes a cook—experienced or novice—feel relaxed and confident, it is having a dinner main dish all done long before the time to serve it.

For the occasions when you need this sort of reassurance, casseroles and meat pies are the answer. Their advance preparation liberates you to enjoy potlucks and carry-in suppers, picnics in the park or at the beach, weekends when the whole family is on the go and you want to go along, or company buffets on days so busy that guests may put in an appearance almost before you do!

In all the following recipes, the point to which the dish may be prepared in advance and then refrigerated is clearly indicated. Remember that if you expect to transfer a container of food directly from the refrigerator to a hot oven, you must be sure to use a baking dish or pan that will withstand such an abrupt temperature change without cracking.

Most made-in-advance casseroles will bake more satisfactorily if you let them stand at room temperature for up to an hour before baking, if your schedule permits. In warm weather, however, it is a wise safety precaution to keep any dish with eggs or a cream sauce cool until you are ready to put it in the oven.

Baking times for dishes to be prepared ahead are approximations that depend on the actual temperature of the food when it goes into the oven. To be sure a dish is ready to serve, check the center by inserting a small sharp knife; if steam rises, it has probably baked enough. If the top or edges become too brown before the center heats through, use a covering of aluminum foil during the last 15 or 20 minutes.

Rolling out the pastry for the top crust of a traditional chicken pie with carrots, peas, mushrooms and a creamy sauce made with the cooking broth (see page 91)

Stuffed Pasta with Tomato Sauce

Many favorite casseroles are made with spaghetti, macaroni or noodles. This one uses the big, fat tubes of pasta called *manicotti*—a natural for meaty stuffing. Both filling and sauce are quick and surprisingly easy to make.

1 package (7½ to 8 oz.) manicotti
Boiling salted water
1 pound ground beef, crumbled
1 large onion, finely chopped
½ cup soft bread crumbs
2 cups shredded Monterey jack cheese
1 teaspoon salt
⅛ teaspoon pepper
1 clove garlic, minced or pressed
1 large can (15 oz.) tomato sauce with tomato bits
1 cup regular-strength beef broth (homemade or canned)
½ cup dry red wine
1 teaspoon crumbled basil
½ teaspoon crumbled oregano
½ cup grated Parmesan cheese

1. Cook manicotti in boiling salted water according to package directions, undercooking slightly. Drain, rinse with warm water and drain again. Separate on paper towels; set aside.

2. In a large heavy frying pan cook ground beef in its own drippings with about half of the onion, stirring until meat is well browned; spoon off most of the fat. With a slotted spoon, remove meat and onions to a bowl; stir in bread crumbs, 1 cup of the jack cheese, salt and pepper.

3. In the same frying pan, cook remaining onion until soft. Stir in garlic, tomato sauce, broth, wine, basil and oregano. Bring to boiling and boil gently, uncovered, 5 minutes. Pour about half of the sauce into a greased shallow 3-quart baking dish.

4. Carefully fill the drained manicotti with the meat mixture. Arrange in sauce in baking dish. Pour on remaining sauce. Sprinkle with remaining 1 cup jack cheese and Parmesan cheese. (At this point, casserole can be covered and refrigerated until ready to bake.)

5. Bake, uncovered, in a 350° oven for 25 to 45 minutes until pasta heats through, sauce bubbles all over and cheese browns lightly.

Makes 5 to 6 servings.

Manicotti are stuffed with ground beef, topped with cheese.

Garden Fresh Spaghetti Sauce

Make this spaghetti sauce in the summer—when the tomatoes in your garden (or the neighbors') ripen all at once—and freeze it for winter suppers.

- 2 tablespoons butter or margarine
- 1 carrot, shredded
- 1 clove garlic, minced or pressed
- 1 large onion, chopped
- 1 pound lean ground beef, crumbled
- ½ pound ground pork, crumbled (*or* use 1½ lbs. ground beef, omitting pork)
- 5 large tomatoes, peeled and coarsely chopped
- 1 can (8 oz.) tomato sauce
- 1 teaspoon salt
- 1 tablespoon crumbled basil
- ½ teaspoon *each* sugar and oregano
- 1 cup dry red wine

1. Heat butter in a large frying pan or Dutch oven; in it cook carrot, garlic and onion until soft but not browned. Add ground meats and cook, stirring frequently, until all the red color is gone from the beef and pork.

2. Stir in tomatoes, tomato sauce, seasonings and wine. Bring to boiling, reduce heat, cover and simmer 1 hour. Uncover and cook over moderate heat for about 1 hour longer, stirring occasionally, until sauce is thick.

3. Salt to taste. Refrigerate, then reheat; or freeze, thaw in refrigerator and reheat to serving temperature.

Makes about 6 cups, or from 8 to 10 servings.

Easy Individual Pizzas

These shortcut pizzas made with English muffins are so speedy there really isn't any need to make them ahead—unless you want to leave them in the refrigerator for a simple do-it-yourself family supper on the cook's night out.

- 1 pound mild Italian sausages
- 1 can (8 oz.) tomato sauce
- 1 can (4 oz.) mushroom pieces and stems, well drained
- 1 clove garlic, minced or pressed
- 2 teaspoons Italian herb seasoning
- 4 English muffins, split
- ½ cup grated Parmesan cheese
- 2 cups shredded Monterey jack cheese

1. Remove sausage casings and crumble meat into a large frying pan. Cook, stirring, until browned; spoon off excess fat. Mix in tomato sauce, mushrooms, garlic and Italian herb seasoning. Bring the mixture to boiling, reduce heat and simmer, covered, 10 minutes.

2. Meanwhile, toast English muffins in broiler until cut sides are browned. Spread each toasted muffin half with sausage mixture. Then top each with 1 tablespoon Parmesan cheese and ¼ cup of the jack cheese. (At this point, pizzas can be covered and refrigerated for several hours until ready to bake.)

3. Place pizzas on a baking sheet and bake in a 450° oven for 10 to 15 minutes until cheese is melted and lightly browned.

Makes 4 servings, 2 pizzas each.

Baked Meatballs in Red Wine

An easy way to make meatballs is to bake them in a very hot oven, rather than browning and turning them individually on top of the range. These baked meatballs, enriched with an elegant wine and mushroom sauce, can be accompanied by hot rice.

- 2 eggs
- ¾ cup soft bread crumbs
- ⅓ cup half-and-half (light cream)
- 1½ teaspoons salt
- ⅛ teaspoon *each* ground allspice and pepper
- 1 small onion, chopped
- 2 pounds ground beef
- 2 tablespoons butter or margarine
- 1 can (4 oz.) mushroom pieces and stems, drained
- 1 clove garlic, minced or pressed
- 1½ tablespoons flour
- 1 cup dry red wine
- 2 tablespoons Beef Concentrate (see page 10), *or* 2 teaspoons beef stock base
- Chopped parsley, for garnish

1. Beat eggs; mix in bread crumbs, half-and-half, salt, allspice, pepper and half of the onion, then lightly mix in ground beef. Shape into golf ball-size meatballs. Arrange in a single layer in a shallow baking pan. Bake in a 500° oven for about 10 minutes, until browned.

2. In a 1½-quart saucepan, cook remaining onion in heated butter until lightly browned. Mix in mushrooms, garlic and flour; cook until bubbly. Remove from heat and gradually stir in wine and Beef Concentrate. Return to heat and cook, stirring, until thickened and bubbling.

3. Transfer meatballs to a 2 to 3-quart casserole. Pour on sauce. (At this point you may refrigerate casserole, covered, for several hours or overnight.) Bake, covered, in a 350° oven for 25 to 45 minutes, until meatballs and sauce are heated through and flavors are blended. Salt to taste. Sprinkle with parsley and serve.

Makes 6 to 8 servings.

Greek Ground Beef and Macaroni Casserole

Macaroni, an exotically spiced ground beef sauce and a creamy topping go together to make an attractive casserole known in Greece as *pastitsio*.

- **2 pounds ground beef, crumbled**
- **1 large onion, finely chopped**
- **1 clove garlic, minced or pressed**
- **1 teaspoon salt**
- **½ teaspoon cinnamon**
- **⅛ teaspoon *each* ground cloves and allspice**
- **1 large can (15 oz.) tomato sauce**
- **¼ cup water**
- **1 package (1 lb.) elbow macaroni Boiling salted water**
- **1¼ cups shredded Parmesan cheese Custard-Cream Sauce (recipe follows)**

1. In a large heavy frying pan or Dutch oven, brown ground beef in its own drippings, stirring frequently. Pour off most of the drippings. Mix in onion and cook, stirring occasionally, until soft. Mix in garlic, salt, cinnamon, cloves, allspice, tomato sauce and water. Bring to boiling, cover, reduce heat and simmer 20 minutes.

2. Cook macaroni in boiling salted water according to package directions, undercooking slightly. Drain, rinse and drain thoroughly again.

3. Spread half of the macaroni in a large buttered baking dish about 13 by 9 inches; sprinkle with ¼ cup of the cheese. Top with meat sauce; sprinkle with ¼ cup more cheese. Cover with remaining macaroni and sprinkle with ¼ cup more cheese. Pour on Custard-Cream Sauce evenly; sprinkle with remaining ½ cup cheese. (At this point, casserole may be covered and refrigerated for several hours or overnight.)

4. Bake, uncovered, in a 350° oven for 45 minutes to 1 hour, until center is hot and top is lightly browned. Cut in squares to serve.

Makes 8 servings.

Custard-Cream Sauce: In a 2-quart saucepan, melt ¼ cup butter or margarine. Stir in 3 tablespoons flour, ¾ teaspoon salt, ¼ teaspoon ground nutmeg and a dash of white pepper; cook until bubbly. Remove from heat and gradually stir in 2 cups milk. Return to heat and cook, stirring constantly, until thickened. Beat 3 eggs in a mixing bowl; using a wire whisk, gradually mix in hot sauce, whisking until smooth and well blended (do not heat further).

Many make-ahead casseroles begin with ingredients you can easily keep on hand; enhance them with fresh vegetables and herbs, ground beef and cheese.

Beef and Sauerkraut Buns

Who does not remember the tempting goodness of freshly baked bread, steamy and fragrant as it comes from the oven, so soft you know you should wait, but too good to resist? Here is a main dish with just such appeal: wheaty pan rolls filled with ground beef and sauerkraut. Made with a refrigerator dough that requires no kneading, the meat-filled buns make a good family supper with milk or beer, crisp vegetables and a dessert of fresh apples and ginger cookies.

1 package active dry yeast
1 cup hot water
¼ cup sugar
¾ teaspoon salt
½ cup (¼ lb.) soft butter or margarine
3 cups unsifted all-purpose flour
1 egg
½ cup graham or whole wheat flour
Beef and Sauerkraut Filling (recipe follows)
2 tablespoons salad oil
Soft butter or margarine

1. Sprinkle yeast over water in the large bowl of an electric mixer; let stand about 5 minutes to soften. Stir in sugar, salt and the ½ cup butter, mixing until butter melts. Add 2½ cups of the all-purpose flour. Mix to blend, then beat 5 minutes at medium speed. Beat in egg, then vigorously mix in remaining ½ cup all-purpose flour and graham flour until well combined.

2. Cover and let rise in a warm place until doubled in bulk, about 1 hour. Punch down, turn dough out on a generously floured board or pastry cloth and roll to a 16-inch square. Cut dough into 4-inch squares. Place 2 to 3 generous tablespoons of filling in center of each square. Bring opposite corners together and pinch to seal.

3. Pour oil into a 13 by 9-inch baking pan. As each square of dough is filled, turn it in oil, placing buns side by side in pan with pinched sides down. (At this point, pan may be covered and refrigerated, 3 to 5 hours or overnight.)

4. Uncover pan, if necessary. Let rise until buns are puffy, 45 minutes to 1 hour. Bake in a 400° oven until well browned, 22 to 28 minutes. Brush tops of rolls with soft butter. Serve hot.

Makes 16 meat-filled buns. 4 to 6 servings.

Beef and Sauerkraut Filling: Crumble 1 pound ground beef into a large frying pan. Cook, stirring, in its own drippings until browned. Spoon off excess fat. Mix in 1 small onion (finely chopped), 1 teaspoon salt and ¼ teaspoon pepper; cook 3 to 5 minutes longer. Remove from heat and mix in 1 can (1 lb.) sauerkraut, well drained.

Beef and Sauerkraut Buns, baked in a wheaty yeast dough, are at their best served warm, fresh from the oven or reheated.

Roll dough out to a 16-inch square; cut it into 4-inch squares. In the center of each, spoon beef-sauerkraut filling.

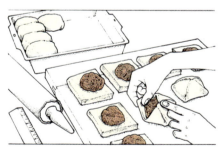

Bring opposite corners of squares of dough to center, pinching edges to seal well. Place filled buns in oiled pan.

Pizza Loaf in French Bread

Another irresistible combination of baked meat and bread is this meat loaf in a hollowed-out loaf of French bread. It makes a good picnic main dish with an antipasto assortment, a red jug wine, and pears and sugar cookies for dessert. If you make it at home to take, first wrap the hot filled loaf tightly in aluminum foil. Then insulate it well with layers of newspaper and it will stay warm for several hours.

1 long loaf (1 lb.) French bread
1 small onion, coarsely chopped
1 clove garlic, minced or pressed
2 tablespoons olive oil or salad oil
½ cup grated Parmesan cheese
1 can (8 oz.) tomato sauce
1 can (4 oz.) sliced mushrooms, drained
¾ teaspoon salt
½ teaspoon crumbled oregano
⅛ teaspoon pepper
1 pound ground lean beef
1 egg, slightly beaten
Soft butter or margarine
2 ounces mozzarella cheese, cut in strips

1. Cut a slice about ½ inch deep from the top of the loaf of French bread. Scoop out most of the bread; tear into small pieces to make 1½ cups; reserve (freeze any extra bread crumbs for other uses, such as in meatballs or meat loaves or to sprinkle over casseroles as a topping).

2. Brown onion and garlic in oil. Mix in reserved bread crumbs, Parmesan cheese, tomato sauce, mushrooms and seasonings. Add ground beef and egg; mix lightly. Spoon into hollowed-out bread shell. Lightly butter outside of loaf. Wrap securely in foil. (At this point, loaf can be refrigerated for several hours or overnight.)

3. Bake in a 375° oven 1 hour and 10 minutes to 1 hour and 30 minutes. Fold back foil; arrange cheese strips over top. Return loaf to oven and bake for about 5 minutes, until cheese is melted and bubbly.

Makes 6 servings.

Stuffed Zucchini Provençale

Meat mixtures also bake well inside scooped-out vegetables, as good cooks in many countries have discovered. Here are zucchini from the south of France, green peppers with a Mexican stuffing and eggplant from Greece.

  6 medium zucchini
    Boiling salted water
  1 pound ground beef, crumbled
  1 medium onion, finely chopped
  1 clove garlic, minced or pressed
  1 can (1 lb.) tomatoes
¼ cup dry red wine
  1 tablespoon tomato paste
  1 teaspoon *each* salt and Italian herb seasoning mixture
⅛ teaspoon pepper
1½ cups shredded Monterey jack cheese

1. Scrub zucchini; cut off stem and blossom ends. Drop into boiling water and cook until barely tender—about 5 minutes. Remove zucchini from cooking water and immerse in cold water; let stand until cool, then drain. Cut in halves lengthwise and scoop out pulp, leaving a ¼-inch-thick shell. Reserve shells and coarsely chopped pulp.

2. In a frying pan brown ground beef in its own drippings over moderately high heat. Mix in onion and garlic, stirring over moderate heat until onion is soft. Spoon off fat, if necessary. Stir in tomatoes (coarsely chopped) and their liquid, wine, tomato paste, and seasonings. Bring to boiling, reduce heat and simmer, covered, 15 minutes. Uncover, add chopped zucchini and cook 15 to 20 minutes uncovered, stirring occasionally until sauce is thick.

3. Heap meat mixture into zucchini shells arranged in a shallow oiled baking dish just large enough to hold them. Sprinkle with cheese. (At this point casserole can be covered and refrigerated until ready to bake.)

4. Bake, uncovered, in a 425° oven for 25 to 35 minutes, until zucchini is tender and cheese is browned.

Makes 6 servings.

Cheese-topped Zucchini Provençale.

Meat and rice mixture fills green peppers.

Stuffed Green Peppers Mexicana

  6 medium-size green peppers (about 2 lbs.)
    Boiling salted water
  2 tablespoons butter or margarine
½ cup slivered almonds
  1 pound ground beef, crumbled
  1 large onion, finely chopped
  1 clove garlic, mashed
⅓ cup raisins
  1 tablespoon cider vinegar
  1 teaspoon *each* sugar, salt and cinnamon
¼ teaspoon *each* ground cumin and cloves
  1 large can (15 oz.) tomato sauce
1½ cups cooked rice (directions follow)

1. Cut a thin slice from stem end of each pepper; carefully cut out seeds. Cook peppers, uncovered, in boiling salted water to cover, 5 minutes; turn upside down to drain.

2. Heat butter in a large frying pan; in it cook almonds until lightly browned; remove from pan with a slotted spoon. In the same pan cook ground beef and onion until lightly browned. Mix in garlic, raisins, vinegar, seasonings and half of the tomato sauce. Simmer, uncovered, about 10 minutes. Mix in rice and almonds.

3. Fill peppers with ground beef mixture. Arrange in an ungreased, deep covered baking dish just large enough to hold the 6 peppers. Pour on remaining tomato sauce. (At this point peppers can be covered and refrigerated for several hours or overnight.)

4. Bake, covered, in a 350° oven 45 minutes; uncover, spoon sauce over and continue baking for 15 minutes.

Makes 6 servings.

To cook rice: In a small saucepan bring to boiling 1 cup water with ¼ teaspoon salt. Add ½ cup short grain or pearl rice. Cover tightly, reduce heat and simmer for about 20 minutes, until water is absorbed.

Baked Stuffed Eggplant

  2 small eggplants, about 1 pound *each*
    Salt
¼ cup olive oil or salad oil
  1 pound ground beef, crumbled
½ cup uncooked short grain or pearl rice
  1 medium onion, finely chopped
  1 clove garlic, minced or pressed
½ teaspoon crumbled oregano
¼ teaspoon cinnamon
¼ cup chopped parsley
  1 can (8 oz.) tomato sauce
    Cream Sauce (recipe follows)
¼ cup shredded Parmesan cheese

1. Remove stem ends of eggplants; cut in halves lengthwise. Score cut sides, cutting to within ½ inch of skin. Sprinkle generously with salt; let stand 30 minutes. Use paper towels to blot moisture from cut surfaces.

2. Heat oil in a large frying pan. Place eggplant halves, cut sides down, in the oil; cover and cook slowly about 5 minutes per side. Leaving the shells intact, cut out eggplant meat with a curved knife; dice it and reserve shells and diced eggplant.

3. In the same pan brown ground beef with rice and onion, stirring until onion is soft. Mix in garlic, oregano, cinnamon, parsley and tomato sauce. Bring to boiling, cover, reduce heat and simmer for about 20 minutes, until rice is nearly tender. Mix in reserved diced eggplant.

4. Divide filling evenly into eggplant shells and place shells in a shallow greased casserole just large enough to hold them. Spread Cream Sauce over the tops of each filled shell; sprinkle with the ¼ cup Parmesan cheese. (At this point, casserole can be covered and refrigerated for several hours or overnight, until you are ready to bake it.)

5. Bake, uncovered, in a 400° oven until sauce is browned and filling is heated through, 25 to 45 minutes. If you wish, cut eggplant halves lengthwise to serve.

Makes 4 to 6 servings.

Cream Sauce: In a 1½-quart saucepan melt 2 tablespoons butter or margarine; stir in 2 tablespoons flour, ⅛ teaspoon nutmeg and a dash of cayenne. Cook until bubbly. Remove from heat and gradually stir in ½ cup *each* regular-strength chicken broth (homemade or canned) and half-and-half (light cream). Return to heat and cook, stirring constantly, until thickened. Cook gently, stirring, for 3 to 5 minutes. Then smoothly mix in ¼ cup shredded Parmesan cheese. Sauce will spread more easily if warm.

Three Pies
from English Pubs

Some of the most typical and enjoyable English food can be found in pubs, especially at noontime, when many of these "public houses" serve well-prepared cold plates, fine cheeses and exceptional meat pies.

The steak and kidney pie is the most formal; accompany it with a green vegetable and a crisp salad. The ham and cheese pie makes a nice brunch or family supper. And the pork pies are the jauntiest of the trio; they are delightful picnic fare with a well chilled English cider or ale.

Steak and Kidney Pie

      6 **tablespoons flour**
 1½ **teaspoons salt**
      ¼ **teaspoons** *each* **pepper and crumbled thyme, chervil, marjoram and summer savory**
      2 **pounds boneless top round, (page 7) cut in ½-inch cubes**
      ½ **pound beef or lamb kidneys, sliced**
      ½ **pound mushrooms, quartered**
      2 **tablespoons butter or margarine**
      ½ **cup dry red wine or regular-strength beef broth (homemade or canned)**
      1 **package (10 oz.) frozen patty shells, thawed (directions follow)**
      1 **egg, beaten with 1 teaspoon water**

1. Mix flour, salt, pepper and herbs in bowl. Mix in round steak cubes and kidney slices to coat well with flour mixture. Sauté mushrooms in butter until lightly browned.

2. Place half of the beef and kidney mixture in a 2-quart baking dish about 2 inches deep. Top with mushrooms, then with remaining meat. Pour on wine or broth.

3. Arrange pastry over steak and kidney mixture; trim and flute edge, sealing it to baking dish. Pierce or slit top in several places to allow steam to escape. Trim with pastry scraps cut into decorative shapes, if you wish. (At this point you may cover and refrigerate the pie for several hours or overnight until ready to bake.)

4. Brush pastry with egg mixture. Bake in a 325° oven for 1½ to 2 hours, until meat is tender (insert a long wooden skewer to test) and pastry is well browned. Serve immediately.

Makes 6 to 8 servings.

To roll out pastry: Arrange the 6 patty shells, overlapping slightly, on a floured board or pastry cloth. Roll out to the shape of the casserole, making the pastry a little larger than the top of the casserole.

Ham and Cheddar Pie

For brunch or supper, serve this pie with fresh fruit, such as pineapple, peaches or berries, for dessert.

1 large boiling potato (about 12 oz.)
  Boiling salted water
1 medium onion, finely chopped
3 tablespoons butter or margarine
¼ cup milk
1 egg
1 teaspoon dry mustard
½ teaspoon salt
⅛ teaspoon ground cloves
4 cups ground cooked smoked pork shoulder picnic, or leftover ham
  Pastry (recipe follows)
  Cheese Sauce (recipe follows)
½ cup shredded Cheddar cheese

I. Peel and quarter potato and cook in boiling salted water to cover until tender, 15 to 20 minutes. Meanwhile, cook onion in butter until soft and beginning to brown. Drain potato well. In a large bowl beat potato with milk until fluffy; then beat in onion mixture, egg, dry mustard, salt and cloves. Lightly mix in ground ham.

2. Line a 10-inch pie pan or quiche dish with rolled-out pastry, trimming and fluting edge. Fill with ham mixture. Top with Cheese Sauce. Sprinkle with shredded cheese. (At this point pie may be covered and refrigerated for several hours or overnight.)

3. Bake on the lowest rack of a 450° oven for 10 minutes. Reduce heat to 350° and continue baking for 25 to 40 minutes longer, until top browns and center is heated through. Let stand about 5 minutes before cutting.

Makes 8 servings.

Pastry: Mix 1¼ cups unsifted all-purpose flour with ¼ teaspoon salt. Cut in ¼ cup firm butter or margarine and 2 tablespoons lard until coarse crumbs form. Gradually mix in 2 to 3 tablespoons cold water, until pastry clings together. Roll pastry out on a floured board or pastry cloth to a circle a little larger than baking pan.

Cheese Sauce: Melt 2 tablespoons butter or margarine in a 1½-quart saucepan. Stir in 2 tablespoons flour and a dash *each* white pepper, nutmeg and cayenne; cook until bubbly. Remove from heat and gradually mix in 1¼ cups milk. Return to heat and cook, stirring, until thickened and bubbly. Stir in 1 cup shredded Cheddar cheese until melted, then mix in 1 tablespoon dry sherry.

Three favorite meat pies of the sort served in English pubs (clockwise from top left): Ham and Cheddar Pie, Traditional English Pork Pies and the savory classic, Steak and Kidney Pie.

Traditional English Pork Pies

The best baking pans for these meaty little pies are straight-sided, deep individual foil pans. Look for them in packages of 8 among the other disposable foil pans at the grocery or hardware store. Bake the pies on a rimmed cooky sheet to prevent drippings from spilling over in your oven.

1 large onion, finely chopped
2 tablespoons butter or margarine
1 clove garlic, minced or pressed
¼ cup brandy (optional)
2 pounds lean boneless pork butt
2 eggs
¼ cup finely chopped parsley
1½ teaspoons salt
½ teaspoon crumbled thyme
¼ teaspoon ground allspice
⅛ teaspoon white pepper
  Pastry (recipe follows)
1 egg, beaten with 1 teaspoon water

1. Cook onion in butter until soft but not browned. Mix in garlic and brandy (if used); continue cooking until onion browns lightly and most of the liquid cooks away.

2. Using the fine blade of a food chopper, grind pork (you should have at least 4 cups). Mix in onions, the 2 eggs, parsley and seasonings. Beat until well combined.

3. Roll out the larger ball of pastry on a floured board or pastry cloth about ⅛ inch thick. Cut into 5-inch circles and press them into 10 individual foil baking pans about 3 inches in diameter and 1½ inches deep. Divide pork filling into the pastry-lined pans. Roll out remaining pastry and cut it into 3½-inch circles. Cover pork filling with top crusts, moistening edges and pressing them together to seal. Cut a small round air vent in top of each. (At this point pies can be covered and refrigerated for several hours or overnight until ready to bake.)

4. Brush top crusts with egg mixture. Place pans on a baking sheet and bake in a 375° oven for about 1 hour and 15 minutes, until well browned. Cool slightly before serving.

Makes 10 servings.

Pastry: Cut ½ cup *each* firm butter or margarine and lard into a mixture of 4 cups unsifted all-purpose flour and 1 teaspoon salt in a large bowl, until mixture is crumbly and forms coarse crumbs. Beat 1 egg in a measuring cup; mix in cold water to make ⅔ cup. Add egg mixture to flour mixture, 1 or 2 tablespoons at a time, mixing lightly with a fork after each addition until the pastry clings together. Use your hands to shape the pastry into 2 balls, 1 twice as large as the other.

Bohemian Cabbage Rolls

Plump cabbage-wrapped packets of ground ham and pork are steamy and good with fluffy white rice.

1 egg
⅓ cup whipping cream
¼ cup soft bread crumbs
¼ teaspoon salt
⅛ teaspoon *each* **ground allspice, dill weed and white pepper**
2 cups ground smoked pork shoulder picnic, or leftover ham
½ pound ground pork
1 large green cabbage
Water
Paprika and flour
2 tablespoons butter or margarine
1 medium carrot, thinly sliced
1 medium tomato, peeled and chopped
1 medium onion, finely chopped
½ cup *each* **dry white wine and tomato juice**
Sour cream and chopped parsley, for garnish

1. For filling, beat egg with cream; mix in bread crumbs, salt, allspice, dill weed and pepper, then lightly combine with ground meats. Set aside.

2. To prepare cabbage, cut out core and carefully separate outer 6 leaves (reserve the remainder for salad or other uses). Cut out thickest part at base of each leaf. Place leaves loosely in a large deep frying pan with just enough water to cover the bottom. Cover and steam for 2 to 3 minutes, just until leaves are wilted and bright green. Remove from pan; drain.

3. Divide filling among the 6 prepared cabbage leaves. For each cabbage bundle, fold in sides, then roll up loosely and fasten with a wooden pick. Sprinkle cabbage rolls lightly with paprika, then coat with flour.

4. Pour water from pan in which cabbage was steamed, and in it heat butter. Brown the cabbage rolls lightly on all sides, transferring them to a 2 to 3-quart casserole as they brown. Surround with carrot and tomato.

5. In pan in which cabbage was browned, cook chopped onion until it begins to brown. Mix in wine and tomato juice. Bring to boiling and cook, stirring, for 3 minutes. Pour over cabbage rolls. (At this point casserole may be covered, refrigerated overnight.)

6. Bake, covered, in a 375° oven for 1 hour. Uncover and continue cooking for 15 minutes longer. Serve cabbage rolls with vegetables and sauce spooned over and topped with a dollop of sour cream and a sprinkling of parsley.

Makes 6 servings.

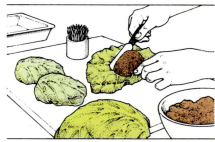

Fill steamed cabbage leaves with ham mixture; fold in sides and roll up.

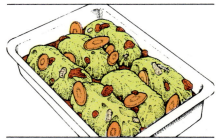

Place carrot, tomato around cabbage rolls.

Ham and Cheese Crêpes

Using crêpes, which can be made ahead and frozen, you can make a versatile entrée baked in a delicate cheese sauce complemented by a moist ham filling.

16 Crêpes, 6 to 8 inches in diameter (recipe follows)
4 cups ground smoked pork shoulder picnic, or ham
1 cup sour cream
3 green onions, thinly sliced (use part of tops)
2 teaspoons Dijon-style mustard
2 tablespoons *each* **butter or margarine and flour**
Dash *each* **white pepper and cayenne**
1 cup milk
½ cup regular-strength chicken broth (homemade or canned)
1 cup shredded Cheddar cheese
1 tablespoon dry sherry
½ cup shredded Parmesan cheese

1. Thaw crêpes, if they were made ahead and frozen.

2. Mix ham, sour cream, onions and mustard. Fill crêpes with ham mixture. Roll up and place, side by side, seam side down, in a buttered baking dish about 13 by 9 inches.

3. For sauce, melt butter in a 1½-quart saucepan. Stir in flour, white pepper and cayenne; cook until bubbly. Remove from heat and gradually mix in

Cabbage rolls are delicious with their sauce spooned over rice.

milk and chicken broth. Return to heat and cook, stirring, until thickened and bubbly. Stir in Cheddar cheese until melted, then mix in sherry.

4. Pour cheese sauce over crêpes; sprinkle with Parmesan cheese. (At this point casserole can be covered and refrigerated for several hours or overnight.)

5. Bake, uncovered, in a 400° oven for 20 to 35 minutes until crêpes are heated through and cheese sauce is lightly browned.

Makes 6 to 8 servings.

Crêpes: In blender container combine 1 cup unsifted all-purpose flour, ¾ cup water, ⅔ cup milk, 3 eggs, 2 tablespoons salad oil and ¼ teaspoon salt. Whirl about 1 minute at high speed; scrape down any flour clinging to sides, then whirl again briefly. Cover and refrigerate batter at least 1 hour. Make crêpes using a lightly oiled 6 to 8-inch pan, stacking them as each crêpe is completed. (Crêpes can be made ahead and frozen, if you wish.)

Crêpes Cannelloni

Crêpes also can be used in place of pasta to make *cannelloni*—a delicate northern Italian casserole with a subtle veal and ham filling and a mild tomato-cream sauce.

1 mild Italian sausage (about ¼ lb.)
1 medium onion, chopped
¼ cup chopped parsley
1 carrot, shredded
1 small jar (2 oz.) sliced pimientos
1 can (1 lb.) tomatoes
1 cup regular-strength chicken broth (homemade or canned)
1 teaspoon crumbled basil
Cream Sauce (recipe follows)
Salt
Crêpes (see previous recipe)
Veal and Ham Filling (recipe follows)
2 cups shredded Monterey jack cheese

1. Remove casing from sausage and crumble the meat. Cook with onion in the sausage drippings in a large frying pan until onion is soft. Mix in parsley, carrot and pimientos; cook about 5 minutes longer. Add tomatoes (coarsely chopped) and their liquid, chicken broth and basil. Bring to boiling, then cook, uncovered and stirring occasionally, at a gentle boil until sauce is thick, about 30 minutes. Cool slightly.

2. Mix tomato sauce with Cream Sauce; salt to taste. Spread in an ungreased, large shallow baking dish about 13 by 9 inches.

3. Fill crêpes, using about ¼ cup of the filling for each. Roll up and place, seam side down, side by side in sauce

in baking dish. Sprinkle with cheese. (At this point casserole can be covered and refrigerated for several hours or overnight.)

4. Bake in a 400° oven for 30 to 45 minutes, until crêpes are heated through and cheese browns lightly.

Makes 8 servings.

Cream Sauce: Heat ¼ cup butter or margarine in a 1½-quart saucepan. In it cook 1 small onion, finely chopped, until soft but not browned. Mix in 3 tablespoons flour and ¼ teaspoon ground nutmeg; cook until bubbly. Remove from heat and gradually stir in ¾ cup regular-strength chicken broth (homemade or canned) and 1 cup milk. Return to medium heat and cook, stirring, until thick.

Veal and Ham Filling: In a large frying pan cook 1 pound ground veal or turkey (crumbled) and 1 large onion (finely chopped) in ¼ cup butter or margarine until onion is soft and meat loses its pink color; mix in 1 clove garlic (minced). Remove from heat.

Using the fine blade of a food chopper, grind 1 cup diced cooked smoked pork shoulder picnic or leftover ham. Mix ground ham with veal mixture, then smoothly mix in 1 cup (½ lb.) ricotta cheese, ½ cup shredded Parmesan cheese, 1 egg, ½ teaspoon salt and ⅛ teaspoon ground nutmeg. Cover the filling and chill until ready to use.

Baked Frankfurters and Lentils

A pleasant change from the usual beans-and-franks combination is this casserole made with wholesome lentils. Accompany with sharp mustard and rye bread.

1 package (12 or 14 oz., about 2 cups) lentils
1 can (1 lb.) tomatoes
1 can (13¾ oz.) regular-strength beef broth
6 slices bacon, cut in squares
½ cup catsup
1 medium onion, finely chopped
1 bay leaf
¼ cup brown sugar
1 tablespoon prepared mustard
2 tablespoons molasses
1 pound frankfurters

1. Rinse and drain lentils. In a 2 to 3-quart casserole, lightly mix lentils, tomatoes (coarsely chopped) and their liquid, beef broth, uncooked bacon, catsup, onion, bay leaf, brown sugar, mustard and molasses.

2. Cover and bake in a 350° oven until lentils are tender, about 2 hours, stirring 2 or 3 times and adding up to 1 cup water if mixture seems dry. (This

much can be done ahead, then refrigerated for several hours or overnight, if you wish.)

3. Using a cooking fork, pierce frankfurters in several places to prevent bursting. Add to lentils, pressing them down into lentil mixture. Cover and continue baking for 15 to 20 minutes longer (up to 1 hour and 15 minutes, if lentils were refrigerated), until frankfurters are heated through. Remove the bay leaf.

Makes 5 to 6 servings.

Lamb and Eggplant Casserole

A generous, crusty Swiss cheese topping gives this vegetable-rich, ground lamb casserole an extravagant finishing touch.

1 large eggplant (about 1½ lbs.)
Salt
½ cup olive oil or salad oil (approximately)
1 pound ground lamb, crumbled
1 large onion, finely chopped
2 cloves garlic, minced or pressed
1 small red or green bell pepper, seeded and cut in strips
¾ teaspoon *each* salt and basil
¼ teaspoon crumbled oregano
⅛ teaspoon crumbled thyme
¼ cup chopped parsley
2 large ripe tomatoes, peeled and coarsely chopped
2 cups shredded Swiss cheese

1. Cut unpeeled eggplant into ¾-inch cubes. Spread in a single layer on several thicknesses of paper towels. Sprinkle liberally with salt; let stand for 20 minutes. Then blot up surface moisture. Heat about half of the oil in a large frying pan over moderately high heat. Add eggplant, about half at a time, and brown on all sides, removing and reserving it as it browns. Add more oil as needed.

2. When all the eggplant is browned, add ground lamb and cook in its own drippings, stirring until browned. Spoon off excess fat, if necessary. Mix in onion, garlic and red or green pepper, cooking until onion is soft. Mix in seasonings, parsley and tomatoes. Cover and simmer 15 minutes. Uncover and continue cooking for 8 to 10 minutes longer, until thick. Mix in eggplant. Cover and simmer for 10 to 15 minutes more, until the cubed eggplant becomes tender.

3. Transfer lamb and eggplant mixture to an ungreased shallow 2-quart baking dish; sprinkle with cheese (at this point casserole can be covered and refrigerated).

4. Bake, uncovered, in a 425° oven for 25 to 35 minutes, until cheese is crusty and well browned.

Makes 6 servings.

A Greek Dinner for Six

Sometimes it's fun to plan a menu around a special ethnic dish, selecting appropriate accompaniments from the cuisine of the same culture. A Greek evening is suggested by the elegant layered lamb and eggplant casserole, *moussaka*.

Lemon and Rice Soup (*Avgolemono*)
Moussaka
Greek Country Salad
Sesame-Seeded Bread   Butter
Baklava
Suggested wine: Retsina,
Zinfandel or Gamay Beaujolais

Lemon and Rice Soup

5 cups Golden Chicken Broth (see page 11), *or* 3 cans (13¾ oz. *each*) regular-strength chicken broth
3 tablespoons uncooked long-grain rice
5 eggs
¼ cup fresh lemon juice
Thin lemon slices

1. Simmer broth and rice, covered, until rice is tender, about 20 minutes.

2. In a bowl, beat eggs until foamy; gradually mix in lemon juice, beating until blended. Pour part of the hot soup slowly into egg mixture, then return to remainder of the soup, stirring constantly. Stir over very low heat until steaming hot, but *do not boil*. Serve at once, garnished with lemon slices.

Makes 6 servings.

Moussaka

1 large eggplant (about 1½ lbs.)
Salt
1 pound ground lamb, crumbled
⅓ cup olive oil or salad oil (about)
1 large onion, finely chopped
1 clove garlic, minced or pressed
¼ teaspoon cinnamon
1 teaspoon salt
⅛ teaspoon *each* nutmeg and white pepper
¼ teaspoon crumbled oregano
¼ cup chopped parsley
2 tablespoons tomato paste
½ cup dry red wine or beef broth
½ cup shredded Parmesan cheese
Cream Sauce (recipe follows)

1. To prepare eggplant, cut off stem end; cut unpeeled eggplant in half lengthwise. Cut crosswise in ½-inch slices. Arrange in a single layer on

Clockwise from top, Greek dinner includes a country salad, honey-and-almond-filled pastries, lamb and eggplant casserole and tart, creamy lemon soup.

paper towels; sprinkle with salt. Let stand while preparing meat sauce.

2. Cook lamb in a large frying pan in 1 tablespoon of the oil, stirring until browned. Spoon off excess fat, if necessary. Mix in onion and cook, stirring occasionally, until onion is tender. Mix in garlic, cinnamon, salt, nutmeg, white pepper, oregano, parsley, tomato paste and wine or broth. Bring to boiling, reduce heat, and simmer, covered, 15 minutes; uncover and continue simmering until sauce is thick, about 5 minutes longer.

3. Blot up moisture from eggplant slices with a paper towel. Arrange eggplant in a single layer in a large shallow pan. Brush with some of the remaining oil. Broil, about 4 inches from heat, about 5 minutes, until lightly browned. Turn, brush second sides with oil, and broil about 5 minutes longer, until browned.

4. To assemble the dish, place half of the eggplant in a single layer in an ungreased 9 to 10-inch square or oval casserole (about 2-quart capacity). Top with meat sauce; sprinkle with 2 tablespoons of the Parmesan cheese. Cover with remaining eggplant; sprinkle with 2 tablespoons cheese. Pour on Cream Sauce; sprinkle with remaining cheese. (Casserole can be covered and refrigerated overnight.)

3. Bake in a 350° oven for 45 minutes to 1 hour, until top is lightly browned.

Makes 6 servings.

Cream Sauce: Melt 2 tablespoons butter or margarine in a medium saucepan; stir in 2 tablespoons flour, ½ teaspoon salt and a dash *each* nutmeg and white pepper. Remove from heat and gradually stir in 2 cups milk. Return to heat and cook, stirring, until thickened. In a small bowl beat 2 whole eggs and 1 egg yolk. Mix in a little of the hot sauce. Blend egg mixture gradually into sauce and mix well over low heat.

Greek Country Salad

6 cups torn iceberg lettuce
2 cups torn curly endive
1 small cucumber, thinly sliced
2 small ripe tomatoes, cut in wedges
⅓ cup Greek olives
4 green onions, thinly sliced (use part of tops)
1 tablespoon drained capers
Herbed Oil and Vinegar Dressing (recipe follows)
½ cup crumbled feta cheese

1. In a large bowl lightly mix iceberg lettuce, endive, cucumber, tomatoes, olives, green onions and capers. Mix in dressing.

2. Top with cheese. Serve at once.

Makes 6 servings.

Herbed Oil and Vinegar Dressing: In small blender container or a tightly covered jar, whirl or shake together ¼ cup olive oil, 1 tablespoon red wine vinegar, 2 teaspoons lemon juice, 1 clove garlic (minced or pressed), ¾ teaspoon salt, ½ teaspoon crumbled oregano and ⅛ teaspoon pepper.

Baklava

Look for the tissue-thin pastry called *fillo* (also spelled *phyllo* or *fila*), refrigerated, in specialty food stores.

½ pound (half of a 1-lb. package) fillo dough
2 cups ground blanched almonds (whirl in blender until powdery)
¾ cup sugar
1 teaspoon grated lemon rind
¾ teaspoon cinnamon
½ pound unsalted butter, melted
Honey and Rose Water Syrup (recipe follows)
Sliced almonds, for garnish

1. Thaw fillo, if frozen (remainder can be refrozen). Bring to room temperature; unfold sheets of dough so they lie flat. Cover with a damp towel, to prevent them from drying out.

2. Mix almonds, sugar, lemon rind and cinnamon. Butter an 8 or 9-inch square baking pan generously.

3. Carefully fold 2 sheets of fillo to fit pan; place in pan 1 at a time, brushing each with butter. Sprinkle about 3 tablespoons of the almond mixture over the top sheet of fillo. Fold 1 sheet of fillo to fit pan; brush with butter. Sprinkle evenly with 3 tablespoons more of the almond mixture.

4. Add more layers, using 1 folded sheet of fillo, a generous brushing of butter and 3 to 4 tablespoons of the almond mixture for each, until nut mixture is used up (you should have about 10 nut-filled layers).

5. Fold remaining 2 to 3 sheets of fillo to fit pan. Place on top, brushing each with butter before adding the next. With a very sharp knife, carefully cut diagonally across the pan to make small diamond shapes about 1½ inches on a side, cutting all the way to the bottom of the pan. Pour on any remaining butter.

6. Bake in a 325° oven for about 45 minutes, until golden brown. Pour warm Honey and Rose Water Syrup over the top. Decorate each piece with an almond slice. Cool before serving.

Makes about 2 dozen pastries.

Honey and Rose Water Syrup: Combine in a 1½-quart saucepan, ¼ cup *each* sugar and water; bring to boiling, stirring. Mix in 1 cup honey and cook until syrup boils again. Remove from heat; mix in 1 tablespoon rose water.

Baked Veal Meatballs with Mushroom Sauce

An accompaniment for these meatballs, sweet potatoes or yams, bakes in the same oven. You might also bake a dessert such as apples—cored, then stuffed with raisins and brown sugar—along with the meatballs.

- **2 eggs**
- **1 cup soft bread crumbs**
- **1 teaspoon poultry seasoning**
- **1½ pounds ground veal**
- **1 medium onion, very finely chopped**
- **2 tablespoons butter or margarine**
- **1 can (10¼ oz.) condensed cream of mushroom soup**
- **⅓ cup dry white wine or water**
- **4 to 6 medium sweet potatoes or yams (see note)**

1. Beat eggs; mix in bread crumbs and poultry seasoning, then lightly stir in veal and chopped onion. Shape into 1½-inch meatballs.

2. Brown meatballs on all sides in heated butter in a large frying pan. Transfer them, as they brown, to a 2 to 3-quart casserole. Pour off the fat. To the same pan add mushroom soup; gradually mix in wine or water, stirring until smooth. Pour sauce over meatballs. (At this point casserole can be covered and refrigerated for several hours or overnight.)

3. Bake, covered, in a 350° oven about 1 hour, until meatballs are browned and bubbling.

Makes 4 to 6 servings.

Note: To prepare sweet potatoes, scrub with a stiff brush, pierce in several places with a fork and rub lightly with butter or margarine. Arrange on oven rack around casserole to bake.

Baked Chicken Savoyard

Few French dishes lend themselves as well to advance preparation as this elegant chicken. Serve with asparagus.

- **3-pound frying chicken, cut up (see page 9)**
- **Salt, white pepper and nutmeg**
- **3 tablespoons butter or margarine**
- **2 teaspoons flour**
- **½ cup *each* dry white wine and half-and-half (light cream)**
- **1 egg yolk**
- **1 tablespoon lemon juice**
- **½ cup *each* shredded Swiss cheese and soft French bread crumbs**
- **1 tablespoon chopped parsley**

1. Sprinkle chicken pieces with salt, white pepper and nutmeg. In a large frying pan, brown chicken in 2 tablespoons of the butter. Remove chicken to a shallow baking dish and arrange pieces in a single layer.

2. Stir flour into pan drippings until bubbly. Remove from heat and add wine and half-and-half, stirring to mix in brown bits. Return to low heat and cook, stirring, until sauce thickens slightly and boils. Meanwhile, beat egg yolk with lemon juice. Gradually stir in a little of the hot sauce. Return egg mixture to sauce; stir in cheese. Cook over very low heat until cheese melts (do not boil). Pour sauce over chicken.

3. Mix bread crumbs and parsley with remaining 1 tablespoon butter, melted; sprinkle over chicken. (At this point, casserole can be covered and refrigerated for several hours or overnight.)

4. Bake, uncovered, in a 375° oven for 30 to 45 minutes, until chicken is done in thickest part (test with a small knife) and topping is well browned. Serve immediately.

Makes 4 to 5 servings.

Spaghetti bakes in a sherried cream sauce in Chicken Tetrazzini.

Chicken Tetrazzini

Created by a legendary San Francisco chef, this combination of poultry and pasta takes many forms. It is at its best—and most economical—when you start with a whole chicken, simmer it in its own broth and then use the broth in the creamy sauce. Chicken Tetrazzini is a reliable dish to make ahead for a buffet and refrigerate.

- **Chicken and Broth (recipe follows)**
- **⅓ cup butter or margarine**
- **1 cup sliced mushrooms**
- **⅓ cup flour**
- **¾ teaspoon salt**
- **⅛ teaspoon *each* nutmeg, white pepper and paprika**
- **1 cup *each* milk and half-and-half (light cream)**
- **½ cup julienne strips cooked smoked pork shoulder picnic, or leftover ham**
- **¼ cup dry sherry**
- **½ pound spaghetti or vermicelli Boiling salted water**
- **1 cup shredded Parmesan cheese**

1. Prepare chicken as directed; reserving broth.

2. In a 3-quart saucepan heat butter and cook mushrooms until lightly browned. Remove mushrooms with a slotted spoon and reserve them. To the butter in the pan add flour, salt, nutmeg, white pepper and paprika; cook until bubbly. Remove from heat and gradually stir in 1½ cups of the reserved strained chicken broth; then mix in milk and half-and-half. Return to heat and cook, stirring constantly, until thickened and bubbly. Mix in chicken, ham, sherry and reserved mushrooms.

3. Cook spaghetti in boiling salted water according to package directions, undercooking slightly. Drain, rinse with hot water and drain again. Mix spaghetti with chicken and sauce. Place in a buttered 3-quart casserole; sprinkle with cheese. (At this point casserole can be covered and refrigerated for several hours or overnight.

4. Bake, uncovered, in a 375° oven until casserole is heated through and top browns, 30 minutes to 1 hour.

Makes 6 to 8 servings.

Chicken and Broth: Cut a 3-pound frying chicken into serving pieces (see page 9). In a large frying pan or Dutch oven, combine with 1 small onion (coarsely chopped), 1 sprig parsley, 1½ teaspoons salt, ⅛ teaspoon crumbled thyme and 2 cups water. Bring to boiling, reduce heat, cover and simmer for about 1½ hours, until chicken is very tender. Strain and reserve broth. Remove chicken from bones in large pieces, discarding bones and skin.

Flaky golden pastry seals in the goodness of Old-Fashioned Deep-Dish Chicken Pie.

Old-Fashioned Deep-Dish Chicken Pie

Another good reason to buy whole chickens is to make this traditional pie with carrots, peas, mushrooms and a flaky top crust.

Simmered Chicken and Broth (recipe follows)
¼ **cup butter or margarine**
1 **small onion, finely chopped**
¼ **cup finely chopped celery**
3 **tablespoons flour**
Dash *each* **white pepper and nutmeg**
½ **cup thawed frozen peas**
1 **can (4 oz.) mushroom pieces and stems, drained**
Flaky Pastry (recipe follows)

1. Prepare chicken and broth as directed.

2. In a 3-quart saucepan melt butter over medium heat. In it cook onion and celery until onion is soft but not browned. Stir in flour, pepper and nutmeg, cooking until bubbly. Remove from heat and gradually stir in the 2 cups reserved chicken broth. Return to heat and cook, stirring, until mixture is thickened.

3. Mix in chicken pieces, carrots reserved from cooking chicken, peas and mushrooms. Salt to taste. Spread chicken mixture in a straight-sided round baking dish about 9½ inches in diameter and 2 inches deep. Place

pastry over chicken mixture; trim and flute edge and cut slits in top for steam to escape. (At this point pie can be refrigerated and baked several hours later or the following day.)

4. Beat egg white reserved from pastry with 1 teaspoon water. Brush over top of crust. Bake in a 425° oven 30 to 40 minutes until pastry is golden and filling is bubbly.

Makes 8 servings.

You might trim crust with a pastry cutout.

Simmered Chicken and Broth: Cut 2 whole frying chickens (about 3 lbs. *each*) into serving pieces (see page 9). In a 5½ to 6-quart kettle or Dutch oven combine chicken pieces, 1 medium onion (chopped), 3 medium carrots (cut in ½-inch slices), 2 sprigs parsley, 1 bay leaf, 1 stalk celery (coarsely chopped), 1 tablespoon salt, ¼ teaspoon crumbled thyme and 1 quart water. Bring to boiling, reduce heat, cover and simmer for about 1½ hours, until chicken is very tender. Strain and reserve broth; measure 2 cups of the broth for pie and freeze remainder for another use. (See additional recipes using simmered chicken on the next two pages.)

Remove chicken from bones, discarding skin and bones; divide it into generous bite size pieces (about 6 cups). Reserve carrots; discard remaining vegetables.

Flaky Pastry: Mix 1¼ cups unsifted all-purpose flour with ¼ teaspoon salt. Cut in 3 tablespoons *each* firm butter or margarine and lard until mixture forms coarse crumbs. Beat 1 egg yolk with 2 tablespoons cold water (reserve egg white to glaze pastry); add to flour mixture and stir with a fork until pastry begins to cling together. Shape with your hands into a smooth ball. Roll out on a floured board or pastry cloth to a circle about 12 inches in diameter.

Moroccan Pastilla

This chicken pie from North Africa is as exotic as the previous recipe is plain. Moroccan restaurants serve small portions of it as a first course, but it also makes a substantial main dish. The pastry is fillo, the same thin dough as used in the *baklava* in the Greek dinner on page 89.

Simmered chicken (see note)
1 cup finely chopped blanched almonds
¼ cup granulated sugar
2 teaspoons ground cinnamon
½ teaspoon ground ginger
¼ teaspoon *each* ground nutmeg and cardamom
1 small onion, finely chopped
1 cup butter or margarine
6 eggs
2 cloves garlic, minced or pressed
1 teaspoon salt
¼ teaspoon pepper
¼ cup finely chopped parsley
½ pound (half of a 1-lb. package) fillo dough, thawed if frozen
¼ cup powdered sugar
Cinnamon, for garnish

1. Prepare chicken as directed, reserving broth for another use.

2. Place almonds in a shallow baking pan in a 350° oven; bake for 10 to 15 minutes, stirring occasionally, until golden brown. Cool. Mix granulated sugar, the 2 teaspoons cinnamon, ginger, nutmeg and cardamom.

3. In a large frying pan, cook onion in 3 tablespoons of the butter until limp but not browned. Meanwhile, beat eggs with garlic, salt, pepper and parsley. Add to onion mixture and cook over low heat, stirring occasionally, until eggs are softly set (as for scrambled eggs). Remove from heat.

4. Melt remaining butter and with it brush a 9-inch springform pan generously. Unfold sheets of fillo dough so they lie flat. Cover with waxed paper, then a damp towel, to prevent them from drying out. Line buttered pan with 1 sheet of dough, allowing dough to extend over edge of pan; brush generously with butter; top with a second sheet of dough and brush it with butter. Fold 6 more sheets of dough to fit pan and stack them one atop the other, brushing each with butter, within the fillo-lined pan.

5. For filling, arrange a layer of prepared chicken, then egg mixture and finally the toasted almonds. Sprinkle sugar and spice mixture over almonds.

6. Fold remaining sheets of fillo dough to fit pan. Reserving 2 of them for topping, stack remaining sheets over almonds, brushing each with butter. Fold edges of fillo extending beyond the pan in toward the center. Top with

Layers of crisp fillo pastry enclose spiced chicken filling.

the last 2 sheets, folded to fit pan and with any protruding edges tucked down inside pan rim. Brush with remaining butter. Using a razor blade or small sharp knife, cut through top layers of dough down to the almonds to mark pie in 8 wedge shapes. (At this point, you can cover and refrigerate the pie for several hours or until you are ready to bake it.)

7. Bake in a 350° oven for 45 minutes to 1 hour, until well browned and heated through. Remove pan sides. Sift powdered sugar, then about ½ teaspoon cinnamon, over pie. Serve the pastilla immediately, cut in the marked wedges.

Makes 8 servings.

Note: Simmer a 3 to 3½-pound frying chicken, preparing it and broth as in recipe for Chicken Tetrazzini (page 90).

Brush each fillo layer with butter.

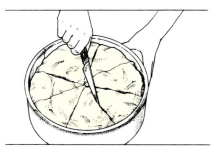

Cut through top layers to make 8 wedges.

Hot Chicken and Green Chile Salad

For a light meal, try this hot chicken salad with a Mexican touch. Accompany it with crisp raw vegetables and beer or iced tea.

Prepared chicken (see note)
½ cup mayonnaise
2 teaspoons lemon juice
1 teaspoon white wine vinegar
½ teaspoon dry mustard
¼ teaspoon *each* garlic salt and ground cumin
1 stalk celery, finely chopped
4 green onions, thinly sliced (use part of tops)
2 canned green chiles, seeded and chopped
½ cup *each* shredded Monterey jack and Cheddar cheese
1 cup crushed corn chips

1. Prepare chicken as directed, reserving broth for other uses.

2. For dressing, mix mayonnaise, lemon juice, vinegar, mustard, garlic salt and cumin until smooth.

3. Lightly combine dressing, prepared chicken, celery, green onions, green chiles and cheeses. Divide the chicken mixture into 4 to 6 buttered shallow individual baking dishes. Top with crushed corn chips. (At this point salads can be covered and refrigerated for several hours.

4. Bake, uncovered, in a 400° oven for 15 to 25 minutes, until salads are bubbly and heated through.

Makes 4 to 6 servings.

Note: Prepare a 3-pound frying chicken, cut up, as in Chicken Tetrazzini (page 90). Divide cooked chicken into bite-size chunks.

Turkey Enchiladas

This meaty main dish makes an attractive choice for a summer evening buffet—with gazpacho, baked red beans and a dessert of sherbet frozen in fresh pineapple halves.

2½ to 3-pound half turkey breast, thawed if frozen
1 can (1 lb.) tomatoes
1 medium onion, finely chopped
1 clove garlic, minced or pressed
1½ teaspoons salt
¼ teaspoon *each* ground cumin and coriander
1 small can (4 oz.) diced green chiles
1 cup whipping cream
12 corn tortillas
1½ cups *each* shredded Monterey jack and Cheddar cheese
½ cup sour cream, mixed until smooth with 2 tablespoons milk
Sliced ripe olives and green onions, for garnish

1. Place turkey breast in a deep frying pan or Dutch oven. Top with tomatoes (coarsely chopped) and their liquid, onion, garlic, salt, cumin and coriander. Bring to boiling, cover, reduce heat and simmer for about 2 hours, until turkey is very tender. When cool enough to handle, remove bones and skin; shred turkey into bite-size pieces (about 4 cups).

2. Bring cooking liquid to boiling; cook, uncovered, stirring occasionally, until reduced to about 2 cups; stir in green chiles. Spread sauce in an ungreased large shallow baking dish (about 13 by 9 inches).

3. Heat cream in a small frying pan. Dip tortillas, 1 at a time, in hot cream until limp. Fill with turkey, using about ⅓ cup for each. Roll tortillas and place side by side in sauce in baking dish. Pour on any remaining cream. Sprinkle with a mixture of cheeses. (At this point enchiladas can be covered and refrigerated for several hours.

4. Bake, uncovered, in a 375° oven for 25 to 45 minutes, until enchiladas in center of dish are heated through and cheese is browned. Spoon sour cream over the enchiladas; sprinkle with olives and green onions and serve.

Makes 6 servings.

Ground Turkey Lasagne

Lasagne seems somewhat lighter and much more subtle when it is made with delicately flavored ground turkey.

2 pounds ground turkey, crumbled
¼ cup butter or margarine
1 large onion, finely chopped
1 clove garlic, minced or pressed
1 can (6 oz.) tomato paste
1 large can (28 oz.) tomatoes
¾ cup dry white wine
2 teaspoons salt
1 teaspoon crumbled basil
½ teaspoon crumbled oregano
¼ teaspoon *each* ground nutmeg and crumbled thyme
½ cup chopped parsley
8 ounces lasagne noodles
Boiling salted water (a few drops of salad oil added)
2 cups (1 lb.) ricotta cheese
3 cups shredded Monterey jack cheese
½ cup shredded Parmesan cheese

1. In a large deep frying pan or Dutch oven brown turkey in heated butter. Mix in onion and continue cooking until soft. Stir in garlic, tomato paste, tomatoes (coarsely chopped) and their liquid, wine, salt, basil, oregano, nutmeg and thyme. Bring to boiling, cover, reduce heat and simmer 20 minutes. Uncover and continue cooking, stirring occasionally, until liquid is reduced by about half, 20 to 30 minutes. Remove from heat, add parsley.

2. While sauce is cooking, cook lasagne in boiling salted water according to package directions, stirring occasionally, until just tender. Drain, rinse with cold water and drain again.

3. In a large shallow greased baking dish about 13 by 9 inches, spread about one-third of the meat sauce; top with one-third of the lasagne, then ⅔ cup ricotta cheese and 1 cup jack cheese. Repeat layers twice, ending with cheeses. Sprinkle Parmesan cheese over top. (At this point casserole may be covered and refrigerated.)

4. Bake, uncovered, in a 350° oven for 35 to 45 minutes until center is heated through and top is browned.

Makes 8 to 10 servings.

Green chiles add a spicy touch to hot chicken salad.

Index

Acknowledgments:
Ann Ashley
Chuck Ashley
Anthony Iacopi
Design Research, Inc.
   for supplying most of
   the props used in
   photographing this
   book.
Tiffany & Co. for the
   table setting, page 12.